Five Virginia Papers

presented at

The Miller Center Forums, 1982

Part II

by

The Honorable Roswell Gilpatric

The Honorable Philip Klutznick

Harry Ashmore

Admiral K. S. Masterson, Jr.

Admiral Harry D. Train, II

UNIVERSITY
PRESS OF
AMERICA

LANHAM • NEW YORK • LONDON

Dedicated

to

The New Chairman

of

The Miller Center National Associates

Mr. J. Wilson Newman

TABLE OF CONTENTS

PREFACE

The Forum Series of the Miller Center is designed to bring together theorists and practitioners in American government in the hope that by their discussion they might help to narrow the gulf separating theoretical and practical knowledge about politics and the American Presidency. The Forums, as do other aspects of the Center's program, seek to address key issues of the presidency. Men and women of broad experience come to the Center to speak on a topic closely related to their professional or public careers. Following their presentations, a seminar comprising former public officials, community and business leaders and a representative group of University scholars pose questions and seek further elaboration of important points in the presentations. The transcript of the discussion is edited and sent to the speakers who review them for clarity and accuracy of statements. In keeping with its public trust, the Center then undertakes to make available the text of the Forums to a much wider audience than the thirty participants attending each Forum.

The value of the Forums rests on two carefully conceived principles underlying the colloquia. First, the Center has been fortunate in bringing to the University of Virginia leaders of the highest intellectual qualities and distinctive political attainments. Guests who have conducted earlier seminars include President Gerald Ford, Secretary of State Dean Rusk, Secretary of Agriculture Clifford Hardin, Secretary of the Navy Paul H. Nitze, Senator Hugh Scott, Ambassador George F. Kennan, Ambassador Hermann Eilts, Professor Louis J. Halle, Najeeb Halaby, Ray Scherer, Jack Valenti, Charles McDowell, Tom Reston, Sander Vanocur, Robert Pranger, McGeorge Bundy, Andrew Goodpaster, Hedley Donovan, Michael E. Sterner, U. Alexis Johnson, Charles Bartlett, Lloyd Norton Cutler, Dean Theodore L. Eliot, Jr., Senator Charles McC. Mathias, Congressman Paul Simon, Secretary of Defense Melvin Laird, Ambassador Ellsworth Bunker and his wife, Ambassador Carol Laise, Admiral Kleber S. Masterson, Professor Jacques Freymond, Graham Claytor, Jr., Robert Komer, Dr. Benjamin Mays, The Hon. Abe Fortas, Roger Morgan and Senator Eugene McCarthy.

The other dimension of the Forums, expressing a second working principle, is the careful selection of the most interested and well-qualified seminar participants. An attempt is made to bring together the ablest University community and business leaders. In the first group, that of scholars, the Center invites men and women drawn from all the major University faculties including Arts and Sciences, Business, Education, Law and Medicine. A special effort is made to include a representative sampling of departments within Arts and Sciences. To illustrate, the quality of the seminars has been elevated by contributors from Virginia's outstanding Department of Government

vii

and Foreign Affairs. Economics, English, History, Religious Studies, Slavic Studies and Sociology have also played an active role. Successive Forum speakers have commented on the high quality of the questions and the seriousness of the intellectual exchange at their Forums. Although individual questioners are not identified, they have regularly included such authorities as the great Jefferson scholar, Dumas Malone; a former Judge of International Court of Justice, Hardy Dillard; a former University President, Edgar Shannon; and a former Virginia Governor, Linwood Holton. Their participation and that of a host of others has assured that the seminar discussions would reach a level of excellence seldom attained in public forums.

At the same time, the presence of thoughtful business and community leaders and former public officials has introduced a breadth of concern and practical insights into the Forums. It would have been impossible for the Forums to have been as broad-gauged and inclusive and to have achieved the quality of concreteness which individual Forums demonstrate if men of practical experience had been absent from the dialogue. We, the leaders of the Center, are convinced that the blending of the approaches of scholars and men of affairs has provided a unique texture to the discussions. In both groups, persons of stature and vision have been identified who have had much to offer. The marriage of theory and practice continues to go on between those who conducted the Forums and the seminar participants as a whole as well as among participants drawn from the worlds of scholarship and of public affairs. What could be more appropriate in "Mr. Jefferson's academical village" in the shadow of Monticello?

INTRODUCTION

The major themes of the Miller Center Forums in the winter and spring, of 1982 followed the main lines and directions established in 1979, 1980 and 1981. In this respect, the nation's political agenda has continued to set the pattern of Forum discussions.

The presidency is the most powerful office in the world, but the demands on the office have vastly increased. The people judge the president as communicator, by the quality of his staff and the consequences of his policies. Not surprisingly in an era marked by crises in confidence in all institutions, problems of presidential leadership stand at the forefront of urgent national issues. The president is buffeted by pressures which make coherent policies difficult. Presidential leadership is many-sided involving the President's role as chief executive and the nation's political leader, head of his own party and leader of a free people in world affairs. The various strands of the President's national and international leadership role interact with one another. None can be ignored at the expense of the others. Not only has America become at the same time stronger yet more vulnerable in its position in the world but so has the office of the presidency. The President must speak for a variety of constituencies at home and abroad; but above all he must be guided by the national interest even when this creates possible tension with subnational groups. Never in history has courage been so clearly the master virtue in American politics, and a President aspiring to greatness must set aside the natural impulse to gain personal popularity at any price. Presidential performance is judged by polls that are relentlessly conducted using questions that may or may not be addressed to the real issues. Thus any President is endlessly confronted by the dilemma of courageously pursuing the national interest or winning success in an unending popularity contest. As with the nation, the presidency is at once the most powerful executive office in the world while at the same time being the most vulnerable to popular pressures. In no area is this dilemma more acute than in defense and economic policy and the conduct of diplomacy. Observers ask whether fundamental measures are called for to strengthen the presidency and to alter the structure of government.

The President's relationships with the Congress constitute a second theme in the nation's political agenda and that of the forums. In the 1980s, these relationships have been complicated by far-reaching changes in the Congress where new centers of power have grown up. More than one hundred and twenty sub-committee chairmen vie with one another seeking to advance their place and position in the political universe. Cooperation has become more rather than less difficult as a result of reforms in the organization of the Congress. Gone are such legendary figures on both sides of the aisle as Speakers Sam Rayburn and Joe Martin whose ultimate goal was working with the President to formulate good legislation. On the side of the presidency, skill and effectiveness in working with the Congress has suffered setbacks in recent administrations. Some critics speak of two separate governments at opposite ends of Pennsylvania Avenue each seeking to rule the nation. Others warn of the threat of a political deadlock. Yet the success of the government depends in the end on executive-legislative relations, and the task of furthering this goal remains an unending requirement of good government.

The organization of the office of the presidency and approaches to policymaking and the ordering of relations with the major departments and agencies of government is another theme central to and recurrent in the Forums. Controversy persists concerning the institutional presidency, and the debate will likely continue through the 1980s. The crux of the argument is whether too many powers and functions of government have been transferred to the White House and whether some of them should be exported back to the major departments. A corollary issue concerns the buildup of large staffs in the executive office with an accompanying decline of influence and authority by officials in the departments. How is the need for coordination at the top to be balanced against the requirement for at least some degree of autonomy in the established departments? The President's role as policymaker is linked with the organization of the presidency. Here as Paul H. Nitze pointed out in Volume I of The Virginia Papers, each President approaches his task in a different way. He organizes the machinery available to him in a manner best suited to his personality, his skills and his objectives. The particular area of policymaking may also determine the use he makes of the several units of government. Policymaking for national security policies may not be the same as for peacemaking in the Middle East. The outside observer has a responsibility, however, to assess and evaluate the strengths and weaknesses of any given approach, and the various Miller Center Forums on policymaking are addressed, whether directly or indirectly, to this issue.

The President must also be judged and his record assessed as political communicator, another recurrent Forum theme. His success as communicator goes to the heart of his relationship with the public and these relationships have undergone a drastic transformation with the revolutionary influence of the mass media. It is not necessary to claim that the "medium has become the message" to perceive that politics in an electronic age has taken on new dimensions. Reports of the President's actions are encapsulated in sixty second film clips and the public has come to depend increasingly on television coverage. Not only is the President judged by the image he projects but the media set their own requirements for what can and cannot be put forth clearly and coherently. It is noteworthy that responsible media officials are themselves engaged in a reexamination of the implications of the mass media for the political process.

No review of the American presidency would be complete without attention to the international setting. The president is a world leader as much as he is the chief executive for policy within the nation. Many of the same problems which arise in the debate over the institutional presidency recur in discussions of his role in international affairs. The President's relationship with his ambassadors--the government's eyes and ears in other countries--is a central question. These relationships are complicated by the intermingling of issues of domestic and international politics and the role of presidential envoys sent abroad to speak and negotiate for the President. New forms of diplomacy--multilateral, summit, shuttle and personal--further complicate the equation as does the proliferation of governmental agencies concerned with foreign policy. The subject calls for continued inquiry and discussion.

It is appropriate that the contributors to the publication of volume XI of The Virginia Papers be concerned with the nation's most urgent problems. Roswell Gilpatric was one of President Kennedy's top defense officials and discusses leadership in national defense. Philip Klutznick, Secretary of commerce in the Carter administration examines structural problems in the world economy and organizing policymaking approaches. Harry Ashmore, who is one of America's most respected civil rights leaders, looks back on the leadership of American Presidents in the vitally important area of civil rights. His evaluation of recent American Presidents will be of particular interest to students of human rights. Rear Admiral K. S. Masterson is uniquely qualified to discuss the relationship of science and national defense priorities. Admiral Harry D. Train, II, who was until recently Supreme Allied Commander of the Atlantic Fleet, combines the strategist's concern with geopolitical factors and the military leader's knowledge of military realities. His call for a national defensive strategy is an appropriate conclusion to the present volume.

AMERICA'S MOST URGENT PROBLEMS

Kenneth W. Thompson

The launching of another volume of <u>The Virginia Papers</u> with the publication of volume XI directs attention to three urgent and paramount problems: national defense, the economy and civil rights. It would be difficult to imagine three areas of more central concern for the survival of the republic. In the present volume, five respected Americans approach these subjects with careful attention to those issues that divide the citizenry in the 1980's.

If any subject looms larger than national defense in the debates of the 1980's, it would be difficult to prove it. Sometime in the late 1970's perhaps spurred on by crises in Iran, Afghanistan and Poland, public opinion shifted toward an emphasis on a greater effort at national defense. In part the shift reflected a genuine concern with lagging defense preparations, but in part it represented a response to a rather emotional national leadership. By 1982, the pendulum appeared to be moving toward a more critical attitude toward massive defense spending.

The Miller Center, in seeking to further understanding on defense issues, invited three leading authorities to discuss the state of the nation's defense. One was a high defense official in the Kennedy administration, another was one of the country's most respected naval commanders and the third was a rear admiral whose scientific knowledge surpasses that of most civilian scientists. The former Kennedy official proved to be critical of certain leading viewpoints in the Reagan administration and more explicitly than any of the others called for a greater effort at arms limitation. The naval commander discovered the greatest national failing in a lack of a strategy that would synthesize political objectives and military means. He also drew a vivid distinction between military men who as operatives conducted military operations with the means at hand and the procurement officials who sought to persuade Congress and the public to add new weaponry to the military arsenals. The rear admiral warned against putting all our eggs in one basket. Weapons that at one moment in military history might appear least vulnerable to destruction could prove most vulnerable in the future.

As one reviews the comments of the three respected military officials, on every contentious issue is clear. Only the Honorable Roswell Gilpatric invites serious attention to the difficult questions of negotiating an arms limitation agreement. The others seem more concerned to urge greater efforts toward a major arms buildup. Admiral Harry D. Train, II, warns that the political and military leadership, however they increase their efforts, will be less than successful if they fail to formulate a strategy, something Americans have rather consistently been reluctant to pursue. Rear Admiral K. S. Masterson guides his readers amd his listeners through a maze of scientific complexities in the difficult sphere of new scientific weaponry.

What the contents of this volume and the topics addressed intend to suggest is that military efforts are not enough. The problems of the nation's and the world economy merit equal attention. The secretary of commerce in the Carter administration is uniquely qualified having achieved an enviable position both as a business leader and a public servant. His discussion has the great merit of suggesting that in the same way military and economic problems cannot be approached as though they existed in watertight compartments, national and global economic issues make up an interdependent whole. Secretary Klutznick also discussed in some detail the organization of the economy and the government to ease economic problems. He makes it clear that he sees a need for more cabinet government than recent administrations have maintained.

The third area of urgent problems with which contributors to this volume are concerned is the moral sphere. Long-time civil rights leader and Pulitzer-prize author Harry Ashmore finds that only a few American presidents, and notably Lyndon B. Johnson, have employed the full weight of their office to further equal opportunity. Ashmore fears not only the gains of the top two-thirds of the black population may be lost in the 1980's but that even graver problems may arise if the one-third who make up the underclass in American society continue in a hopeless and desperate condition.

Not every American would agree that the three problems which form the central concerns of this little volume have equal importance for the future of the nation. Some would place one or the other well above all the rest in importance. Yet few would argue that the security of the nation and its common defense, the economic well-being of its people and the moral fabric of the society were not deserving of the most thoughtful attention.

Not everyone will agree with the judgments which follow on security, the economy and civil rights. The issues that arise in all three areas are so large and portentous that an ongoing national conversation such as that which went on at the founding of the republic on these and other topics is needed. By singling out the three urgent problems for discussion, what our five guests have begun a dialogue. It would be my hope that future volumes of The Virginia Papers would add to the conversation.

THE PRESIDENT:
LEADERSHIP IN NATIONAL DEFENSE

Roswell Gilpatric

NARRATOR: We are pleased to welcome you to a Forum with Roswell Gilpatric, deputy secretary of defense from 1961 to 1964. Mr. Gilpatric was also under secretary of the Air Force in the early 1950s. He's a partner of Cravath, Swaine and Moore. He has been a trustee of numerous important groups in New York, vice chairman of the board of trustees of the Metropolitan Museum, and on the board of the New York public library. He's been a director of CBS and Eastern Airlines. He's been active in the Council on Foreign Relations and the Rockefeller Special Studies Project. He is a graduate of Yale, both as an undergraduate with highest honors and a graduate also of the law school. He has honorary degrees from such institutions as Franklin and Marshall, and Bowdoin College. He has played a very active role in the corporate world having been a member of and indeed chairman of the board of Aerospace and of the Fairchild Camera and Instrument Corporation, and other leading corporations.

In the first years of the Kennedy administration, when Americans witnessed a rather exceptional flow of talent to Washington reminiscent in many ways of the flow of talent that came to Washington in the early days of the Roosevelt administration, Mr. Gilpatric was one of those who attracted most attention in that world that brings together policymakers, scholars, and business leaders. One of your predecessors here, Tommy the Cork, referred to the first thousand man down, which he said was the critical determinant in any administration's success. It was remarked that one such person was Roswell Gilpatric, and his presence was a good omen for the Kennedy administration.

Many of you have read the _Time_ magazine account or the _New York Times_ account of the statement on the Cuban missile crisis by the six Kennedy officials who participated in that decision. The statement is a measured and thoughtful one. It offers lessons about the use and the deterrence of the use of force. It has a lot to say about strength, but also about restraint in foreign policy. So for all of these reasons and because Roswell Gilpatric has been a close personal friend of a number around this table, we're delighted to have him with us. We're looking forward to our conversation with him on the President and national defense issues, and we're particularly happy that he will introduce the discussion with comments of whatever length he may choose.

MR. GILPATRIC: In this academic setting I think I should admit to one of my failures. I started out in life trying to be a teacher. I

1

was an instructor in nineteenth century English poetry at Yale. I was not a success. The English faculty did not feel that I had the potential so I had to go to law school to make a living. Anyway, I've always had the thought that maybe I would go back sometime to some campus and try my hand again. I thought I would start out this morning by some comparisons as to how a President, and I'll take President Kennedy and President Reagan as examples, goes about addressing himself to his responsibilities in the areas of international security. In my observation there are two major factors that he has to accept and cope with at the beginning. Obviously, one is the state of American public opinion. And American public opinion as far as defense issues are concerned was quite different in 1960 than it was in 1980. It's true that Kennedy campaigned on a hypothesis, which turned out not to be the fact, that there was a missile gap confronting the United States and that the Soviet Union had not only achieved equivalence with the U.S. in nuclear weapons but it had passed us. Once we got into office we found out that just the opposite was the case in 1961. Because there wasn't any feeling of urgency either on the part of those who were in the administration or American public opinion generally, we were able to do just the opposite of what's happened today. In the first six months we cancelled out three major weapon systems.

It's interesting to note what they were. We cancelled something called the Mobile Minuteman. That was the concept whereby you take these intercontinental ballistic missiles and move them around on railroad cars and trucks, the very same concept that the MX missile started out with fifteen or twenty years later. Another program we cancelled was the Skybolt. The Skybolt was a concept of a space vehicle from which you would launch nuclear weapons. I didn't welcome the idea of carrying nuclear conflict to outerspace then and I don't today. But that was one of the projects the military had under development and we cancelled it out. A third major weapon system cancellation was the B70. The B70's gone through several lives, too. It now is the B1. It reemerged and was resurrected during the Carter administration and he cancelled it and now it's going full-blown at the cost of many billions of dollars.

But coming to the present time, there was no question in my mind at the time of the 1980 election that there was a broad national consensus that we had fallen behind, and we weren't strong enough, and that an increase in military spending was needed. And that cut across both parties. You remember that Carter started out his administration in 1977 with the objective of cutting defense spending. One of my former colleagues, Harold Brown, was then the secretary of defense. By 1979 Carter had reversed himself and actually, if he would have been elected in 1980 instead of Reagan, I doubt if military spending at the present period--I'm not talking about what happens if these increases that are being proposed go through--wouldn't have been much different from what it is today.

2

I've often wondered what are the causes of this change in public opinion. Maybe the concern about our defense capabilities was stimulated in part by the failure of the Iranian hostage effort, the rescue mission, or in part by the seeming inability of the Western world, the U.S. in particular, to do anything about the Soviet invasion of Afghanistan or the repression in Poland. And then we've seen certainly in the Falklands, in Lebanon, and in the current war between Iran and Iraq demonstrations of the fact that military power still can affect the outcome of international security disputes. On the other hand, it seems to me, as an outsider to the administration of course, that there has been a growing concern, not only about the nuclear arms race as evidenced in the support of the nuclear freeze and other arms reduction proposals, including those of the President himself, but also whether we should increase our defense spending to the tune of fifty percent over the next three or four years, taking instead of five and a half percent of the gross national product maybe as much as eight or eight and a quarter percent while we're running tremendous deficits and while we're cutting back on social programs. If I were taking a measurement of the national pulse today, from where I sit, I would say that there's some diminution in this consensus that existed at the time of the 1980 election.

The second factor which confronts a President as he addresses the question of what his defense policy should be is the U.S. military establishment. The U.S. military establishment, as you all know, is the largest single institution in the government of this country. It has more people, it's spent more money, it has lines of communication running not only to the Congress but to the defense industry, and believe me the catch phrase "the military-industrial-congressional complex" is a reality, not just a slogan. For example, when I was in the government, two-thirds of the congressional staff members on the House and Senate appropriations committees and military affairs committees were military reservists. That is to say they were attached to some unit: Marines, Air Force, Army, Navy; they were on government payroll in that capacity, one might say double dipping, but that gave the military department a wonderful access and line of communication to the congressional committees. I found right away that it wasn't enough just for McNamara to go up and sit down with Senator Russell, or Senator Stennis or George Mahon in the House, I had to go around and talk to all these congressional staff people because they were the ones that formulated most of the positions. And any administration which thinks that it can proceed independently of this very strong base of support that the military establishment has, is deluding itself.

That, as I say, is the background of the situation that an administration faces. Of course the first move that a President makes is to pick who are going to be his principal advisors in the national security area. And it's interesting over the years to see how the balance of power in that group from the secretary of state to the secretary of defense and national security advisor, the head of the CIA, the head of the Arms Control and Disarmament Agency, how that shifts.   There are periods, for example, when during my time with the Kennedy administration Robert McNamara definitely had a primary role, a primary voice.   It wasn't that he out-pointed Dean Rusk, but Dean Rusk felt that McNamara was such a strong advocate of his views, was so effective in articulating them and he in effect let the primary role be occupied by McNamara.   And I think you have the same thing true today with Weinberger.   Weinberger seems to have the closest access to President Reagan and he's succeeded in prevailing against other dissenting voices in getting his programs approved.   Whether that will continue once Schultz, who used to be his boss at the Bechtel Corporation, takes hold and whether Schultz will ultimately take a more important voice on broader questions that affect both Defense and State remains to be seen.

Of course there have been eras--certainly Dulles under Eisenhower and Kissinger under Ford and Nixon, except when Kissinger was being challenged by Jim Schlesinger until Jim was fired by Ford--those are periods where the secretary of state dominated the scene in this area.   Then there have been other eras--when I was under secretary of the Air Force under Truman, you had a shared responsibility.   Acheson was very strong, enjoyed great confidence in the President.   At the same time General Marshall, followed by Bob Lovett, enjoyed the same intimacy and confidence of the President. And during the Carter administration Cy Vance and Harold Brown also shared that.

Another important element in this equation of who influences the President the most is the occupant of the position of national security advisor.   And we have seen some very assertive types.   In my day it was Mac Bundy, followed by Walt Rostow.   Henry Kissinger was no shrinking violet when he was there, and Zbig Brzezinski followed in his steps.   On the other hand you've had some low key types.   Sid Souers was under Roosevelt; Bobby Cutler and Andy Goodpaster under Eisenhower; General Scowcroft, for whom I have great admiration, under Ford; and I gather today that Judge Clark is not the aggressive type, he's more of a low key type.   I think of all of Reagan's appointments, the ones that give me the greatest pause, not for any personal reasons because a number of them are good friends of mine, are in the arms control and disarmament area.   You have a group of people who are hard-liners to a man.   There isn't one of them who either philosophically or ideologically really believes in arms limitation and control.   Most of them believe, because I've heard this directly from one of them, that a Third World War is inevitable; whether it's fought in space or on the ground is a matter of timing and what happens to technological development.

4

But whether it's Paul Nitze, who I went to school with, or Gene Rostow whose class I used to teach at Yale, or General Romny, Burt in state, Ikle in Defense, Perle in Defense--they all give the President one point of view, as I observe it as an outsider. And that does give me some concern because I feel that, in sitting down as we are doing today in Geneva in two different forums, one on the zero option proposal for European based intermediate range missiles or the START proposal with one third reduction in warheads and land based and sea based missiles, you've got to overcome what I would think would be a skepticism on the part of our counterparts across the table, the Soviet Union, as to how really genuine a desire there is on the part of the present administration to achieve some lessening of this nuclear escalation. And I think it's particularly significant that the one area where the United States is clearly and demonstrably ahead in arms development today are cruise missiles. Cruise missiles, whether they are launched from a sea based platform or whether they are launched from some air carrier, strategic bomber or some other air carrier, will probably be a major factor in the arms equations between the Soviet Union and the U.S. in another five to ten years. There's no question that the Soviet Union is more concerned about our position in cruise missiles. But the Reagan administration, as you all know, wants to go ahead with the MX, wants to go ahead with the Bl, with the Stealth bomber, wants to add a hundred and fifty ships to the Navy, wants to add three more Army divisions; they want to add four more tactical wings, and that all will result in a total force that will be over two million two hundred thousand.

As you all know, we've barely been able to maintain in the past decade strength of two million without a draft. In other words, we've increased military pay, and in periods where the jobless are numerous, the armed forces have been able both to recruit and retain the necessary personnel, but there have been periods when naval ships haven't been able to leave Norfolk and where flying time for the Air Force has been curtailed because they don't have mechanics. The skills to retain are just as important or more important than gaining the recruits. I think it's clear that the country today wouldn't support a reintroduction of military conscription, even though some of us may believe philosophically that we ought to have some sort of universal manpower service obligation in this country. Without an extraordinary act of national leadership to bring about the necessary changes in public opinion I don't think you could reintroduce the draft. So I don't see down the road we are going to add to the overall dimensions of our armed forces, our active duty forces, by two or three hundred thousand positions. How are we going to be able, with a shrinking manpower pool, even to maintain those levels.

Coming back to the nuclear equation between the Soviet Union and the United States--it's obviously one of the first things that a President has to look at before he can come up with a strategic doctrine. He's got to assess what the risks are, what are the military risks confronting the United States, to provide against which forces should be maintained. After World War II the common formulation up until the Sino-Soviet split was that the United States might have to face at any one particular point of time two major wars, one in the Far East initiated by communist China, and one in Europe initiated by the Soviet Union with lesser scale of engagement in the Middle East, Persian Gulf, or South East Asia, along the lines of the Korean and the Vietnam wars. I'm not saying that the administrations that were in power during that time necessarily provided the forces that would meet with those contingencies, but at least that was the formulation of what we had to deal with.

Then of course after the Sino-Soviet split, the formulation changed to a one and a half war contingency. Now we have a new formulation, a so-called global threat, the rationale for which is that the United States must be prepared to meet Soviet aggression at any point in the globe, on any one of the seven seas or the three oceans we must be prepared to deploy our fleets and that's why of course we need six hundred ships instead of four hundred and fifty ships. So in other words, the global threat is coupled with what you might call a geographical escalation, a maritime strategy, which is a quantum jump in what the United States should take on. I'm glad to see at least Clark on one occasion said that he thought the U.S. could not be the policeman of the world. You have to have some priorities, which is really what we've been doing ever since World War II. We've accepted our worldwide responsibilities but we've had the Nixon doctrine and this doctrine and that doctrine; we've had various limitations that have been dictated by the necessities of the situation.

But some other developments, too, give me some pause. The concept that nuclear forces have as their sole objective deterrence, each side having enough force to deter the other from initiating a nuclear war, has been augmented by the idea that you could fight and win nuclear wars. Actually Mr. Weinberger didn't invent this idea. Jim Schlesinger, before he left, had a kind of counterforce theory whereby you would have enough nuclear forces so you could absorb a first strike from the Soviet Union and still have enough missiles or other nuclear weapons left to go on and prevail in a nuclear conflict. I never in my thirty years of experience in this part of our national affairs have been able to conceive of anybody winning a nuclear war, nor have I been able to comprehend how you could fight a limited nuclear war, which is another concept that has some support.

Certainly the one thing we don't need is any kind of a major conflict today. I've believed for many years that we've reached a point technologically in our armaments where military force alone does not provide solutions. Maybe it does in a local conflict such as the Falklands or as we've seen in Lebanon--there are always going to be

6

local wars--but not the kind of major confrontation that would be involved if the U.S. and the Soviet Union ever came head on. It ought to be the overriding objective of any administration to do everything possible in protecting our security to make nonconfrontation possible.

There are two other developments that I might mention in my preliminary remarks and that is for the first time in twenty years the administration is reintroducing civil defense as a major activity, planning for the mass evacuation of people from urban centers. To me that is a portent perhaps of our reversing the ban which the Soviet Union and the United States agreed on ten years ago to outlaw antiballistic missile systems. This may be an unbased fear on my part, but when you couple that with the emphasis I mentioned on space weapons and space systems--the United States Air Force, my old service, has just established a space command and there's no question that the Soviet Union will develop a capability for antisatellite weapon systems, and that we will, too--when you put all these new weapon systems that we're working on, forget for a moment the impact on our economy, the cost implications, take the total effect of it, aren't you destabilizing the kind of environment that we need if we're going to avoid war in the future?

We went through this not too many years ago when the United States solved the problems involved in having multiple warheaded missiles, the MIRVing of our missiles. At that time if we had come forward with a proposal--since the Russians didn't have it just the way they don't have the lead today in cruise missiles--if we came forward with a proposal of self-denial on our part instead of going ahead with MIRVing our entire ballistic missile inventory, we might have avoided what subsequently happened, which is that the Russians of course in due time acquired the same technology. Now their missile forces are MIRVed.

And regarding the proliferation of new weapon systems, unless there's an absolute gap in our arsenal which has to be filled, I don't think today that the Triad concept of having three kinds of nuclear weapons capability is as important. You don't have to take out targets or kill people three times. I don't think you necessarily need for the future the entire capability in every one of these areas. That's why I don't see the need for the Bl bomber. I would go ahead with the Stealth bomber because that involves a whole new technology of nondetectability which is very important in the air as well as in the sea.

So my concern today is that in the next two years of this term of President Reagan's he will listen to some voices outside the circle of advisors he's had around him. He's shown flexibility in other efforts--we had a tax increase bill after a tax reduction bill last year. One of the points on which I admire President Kennedy and President Truman, the two Presidents with whom I had the closest personal contact in my government service, was they always sat around a table like this in a cabinet room or the Roosevelt room, and brought in a whole spectrum of points of view. General LeMay, for example, was always asked his views whether it was in regard to Vietnam or Laos or the Cuban missile crisis. I knew in my bones that the President wasn't going to follow General LeMay's advice; he wasn't going to bomb Cuba back to the stone age, you know. But he listened to the General and the Admirals. And also he listened to people, the Adlai Stevensons; he had a whole galaxy of advisors that he heard out. I feel that's a responsibility that a President has today even though governmental staffs have grown. When I was in the Truman administration the White House staff consisted of thirty five people. Today it must be five hundred and sixty five, or something like that. So it's hard for others to have contact with the President; there may be the variety of viewpoints but I certainly would feel more comfortable if the President reached out and at least listened to some different opinions.

NARRATOR: May I say before we begin the questions that the Yale English department obviously used poor judgement. Who'd like to ask the first question?

QUESTION: Do you have any grounds for optimism at all in view of the fact that we do have a hard-line administration, from the President on down to the disarmament agencies and so on, and a President who will apparently not listen to contrary advice; do you have any hope at all?

MR. GILPATRIC: I do because from what I've known of Secretary Schultz, I've seen him over the years, not close to him but close enough that I think he's a man of very balanced judgement, very deliberate analysis, very strong and I have hopes that he will come to exercise a very primary role among the President's advisors. I've been an admirer of Weinberger for a long time. He did a good job as secretary of HEW, he did a good job in OMB but I just feel that some other voice ought to be reaching the President. So that's the encouragement I find in the present scene. I think with all due respect to General Haig, he wasn't capable of providing this voice of moderation which I think will come from Schultz.

QUESTION: Security force is as much a state of mind as well as weapons systems--is there any chance that the administration might possibly be able, perhaps with some help from Mr. Schultz, to re-evaluate the concept of threat? It is important to look into thinking about security and to begin to think about the kinds of systems, economic and political, that might reduce the sense of threat rather than to look at it so heavily from the point of view of weapons systems and similar military capabilities.

MR. GILPATRIC: I share the thought behind your question, that political, economic, educational, and mercantile relations between the two great superpowers could have a moderating effect. I have grave reservations about the present attitude of the administration, for example, on the Siberian gas pipeline or on the idea of trying to cut off all credit to the Soviet Union from Western Europe while at the same time, of course, we're busily selling them grain whenever they want to buy it. I'm not objecting to that. I would like to see more and more contacts between the two great power blocs on a basis other than just matching each other in weapons. You remember President Kennedy's American University speech. He expressed the hope that we could get away from just this eyeball to eyeball military kind of equation.

I think the world, being what it is today, we're all so interdependent, we've got to think of the Third World, we've got to have some energy and resources left for things other than just huge weapon systems. For example, the average over-run on procurement contracts is about thirty-two percent. That may be evidence that contractors are buying in to get the job, maybe that the Air Force and the Navy are making too many changes or there's too much time elapsed and too much inflation. But the weapons business is a terribly expensive business and it is taking resources away from the kinds of things that would advance other forms of rapport and accommodation.

QUESTION: I wonder if we shouldn't start with something very basic in all these discussions and that is with war itself. Mankind unhappily is something of a predator and I think you have to start with the question: Are there going to be wars or aren't there going to be wars? From the study of history and human nature, so long as there are serious differences of opinion that can't be otherwise resolved, I wonder if they are not going to be resolved by force. That is item one. Item two is, if that premise is right, then the only way to avoid war is to be prepared, or rather the way to preserve the peace is to be prepared for war, as many have said. And with a hundred and fifty flags, or whatever the membership of the United Nations, it grows every day, it would be hard enough if there were just two. And when you have that many people with different ideas, different cultures, different backgrounds, different values, different cultural systems, different everything, it is difficult for me to see how you can avoid sometimes resorting to force, which mankind has done as long as we can tell. And if that is so, then the only way to deter war is to be stronger than the other guy and that of course has happened in our lifetime right now, since World War II. The only reason that we haven't had a war with the Russians is because they are afraid of us and we're afraid of them. So long as we remain afraid of each other there's not going to be any war. And there are a whole lot of other things, but may I ask your opinion on that very fundamental consideration.

MR. GILPATRIC: I would start out by accepting as a fundamental premise that we have to have some kind of rough parity or substantial equivalence in military power even if we don't use it. We can't invite aggression by having the equation so lopsided that it's an invitation to the leadership of other countries to take advantage of that. But granted we need to have that power in reserve, and you can argue about how much power you need, what forms it should take which is what I have been talking about earlier, I still think that when it comes to the use of power, that is where mutual self-restraint can be achieved. The Cuban missile crisis referred to was, I think, a classic example because we had at that time a nuclear superiority. We had a conventional advantage because the confrontation was ninety miles off the southeast coast of the United States. Within reach of our air forces and our landing craft and our naval vessels, we had both conventional and nuclear superiority. The great debates that went on during those ten days were over how much force we would use. And some people for whom I have great admiration, like Dean Acheson, got so exasperated with this idea that we weren't really going to show our power that he walked out of the meetings. He couldn't take it any more. I'm glad to say he came back and went over and persuaded de Gaulle that it was the right thing later on. I felt then as I feel today that the amount of force that you bring to play in any kind of a crisis should be very carefully regulated and controlled. Maybe another time we won't have the opportunity to think it out.

On that subject I might just mention one Pentagon aspect of the Cuban missile crisis to show how fortuitous it was that we weren't faced with a situation where the Soviets had completed the installation of the missiles and the introduction of nuclear weapons into Cuba. During late September and early October 1961 we had very bad weather, flying weather. Then there was a dispute between the Air Force and the CIA over who would fly the U2 missions. And I had endless arguments with Pat Carter, who was then the deputy director of CIA. The Air Force had many more pilots, training, support, more U2s, but the CIA had invented the U2 and they felt they should do it. Finally Mac Bundy stepped in and we began flying the missions, including the mission on October 14 which uncovered the problem. Even then they were camouflaging the installations so that it was only a matter of days before we would have been presented with a _fait accompli_. Now, what would have been the reaction of any government or the American people if the Soviet Union was able to say to the world, "We have intermediate range ballistic missiles in place in Cuba, warheads in place, and you, Mr. United States, you'd better pull your missiles out of Turkey and Italy; you've got to do this, you've got to do that, you've got to pull out of Berlin." I don't think that with that kind of a choice we could have restrained ourselves to the extent that we did. We got there just in time--the timing of these crises coupled with the decision on how much force to

10

bring to bear is what I think is the critical thing, not the possession of the power. I think we have to have that.

QUESTION: Something you mentioned earlier is the key to a point I would like to emphasize. Restraint of strength. It involves two things. One is, first, you have the strength, otherwise you can't show restraint. I think that kind of thing is basic. So what you get back to is the wisdom of highly fallible men to do this. Like everything else, the trouble with the world today is this: deviation from standards is all right, that's good but you've first got to have standards to deviate from. And I think the two things we did recently indicates poor application of strength.

In Vietnam, in my humble opinion, we should have gone in there and just destroyed everything we could, then give a note to the Russians that they can't do this kind of thing and say O.K., it's your country and then we get out, leave it alone, but we didn't do that.

The other point I think is silly; you can't limit warfare. Warfare, as you know very well, the purpose of warfare is to destroy, completely destroy the enemy's will to resist. If that is your effort, if that is what war is about then you have two things-- first, try hard not to get into wars. First, you try to avoid confrontation but if you get into a war, all is fair and the purpose is to destroy the enemy's will to resist and you go and do it as quickly and completely as you can. And nobody's going to win, I recognize that. War is horrible and the people involved in it know it better than anybody else. However, it also seems to be necessary, not necessary but unavoidable. So there is a dichotomy that you have to work out. You get right back to who's making the decisions on that very delicate balance between restraint and strength.

MR. GILPATRIC: The point of view that you express is felt by many patriotic and loyal Americans and many well informed people and I would be the last to characterize it as an unreasonable, irrational position. Personally, to the extent that one can do anything to see that we exercise restraint, it is to put in positions of power in this government people who don't want to see this holocaust happen. I saw some statistics the other day, I think it was one of Admiral Gaylor's newsletters, that we have seventeen thousand nuclear warheads. These are of all categories. There are atomic demolition weapons, tactical bombs, ballistic missiles, you name it, and the Soviet Union has twelve thousand warheads, or so our intelligence people think. Just think of the destructive power of twenty thousand warheads and what we did to Nagasaki and Hiroshima with two twenty-five kiloton bombs. So at some point maybe it's a matter of faith, a matter of hope rather than just cold hard reason, but I do think it behooves us that more people think about these things.

11

There are some very extreme disarmament proposals. I don't have time today to go into them, whether you have the no first use proposal, the bilateral negotiated verifiable nuclear freeze, or the merits of Reagan's START, and zero option proposals. There must be twenty different proposals I've seen about in different forms. So there's a lot of thinking being given to that. At the same time, there shouldn't be any drastic change in our priorities. Looking ahead to 1984, for example, I think no matter who is elected, whether Reagan is reelected or another Republican or whether Kennedy or Mondale or John Glenn, I don't think you're going to see a major change in the thrust. You may not have as many new weapon systems, maybe you'll cancel out a few the way we did when the Kennedy administration came in. But there's too much momentum, as I said earlier, in existence in the U.S. military establishment today and the support it enjoys among the American people and Congress. As I said in response to another question, I don't want to sound apocalyptic or that I've given up hope, because I haven't. I think it's well for us all to think these unthinkable thoughts.

QUESTION: I would like to bring in the dimension of our alliance, NATO alliance and public opinion in other countries of the alliance. In my mind one of the most ominous things you have said is your view of the real positions of our chief negotiators on disarmament. First of all, I too know Gene Rostow, Paul Nitze and others. It's hard for me to accept that these men would take on these jobs in an insincere way. If they do, the whole thing is just sort of a put-on negotiation to pacify public opinion. And surely that perception is going to affect our alliance, in a way, more quickly in France, Germany, Great Britain, more quickly than public opinion here. They'll see through it more quickly.

MR. GILPATRIC: I agree.

QUESTION: What can we do about that? If that is your perception of what they're trying to do or trying not to do, if it's true then how can we defend ourselves to our allies?

MR. GILPATRIC: I wasn't implying that they are insincere. I think they believe that we should hold out for the proposals that we've put on the table: the START proposal of reducing our land and sea based missiles by one third roughly--this was a position which had been approved by the Joint Chiefs of Staff and everybody else who had been consulted. It is quite possible that it could prove to be a nonstarter with the Soviet Union because it doesn't touch strategic bombers, it doesn't touch cruise missiles, and it calls for reductions in areas where they are the strongest at the moment. If there's a window of vulnerability, it is certainly in the capacity of the SS17s, 18s, 19s. We can't expect them to make all the sacrifices. I would hope that we would do as we did in SALT I and SALT II. We evolved some fall-back positions, contingency plans. And I would hope, for example, that the President would regenerate the general advisory commission that Jack McCloy used to head. And you would get from that people from communities like this in the academic world as well as the political world and the military world, you would get some input feeding into the channels around the President on some of the alternatives. But I don't think we could hold the alliance together if we don't make a bona fide effort to reach a negotiating point.

QUESTION: Do you think we've gotten to the point of knowing whether there are negotiating positions?

MR. GILPATRIC: Apparently these things go on and on. I don't know enough; I've not been across the table except in one instance, when I was sent up by President Kennedy with George Ball to get the Soviet Union to take the IL28 bombers out of Cuba. You remember that after we got the missiles out, there were these tactical bombers that could come across and bomb Charlottesville, for that matter. And we had to get those out, obviously. We spent ten days and I remember listening to Mr. Kuznetsov and Mr. Zorin day after day, hour after hour, like collective bargaining with a very intransigent management or union--you couldn't see any daylight for days. When you're dealing in this Geneva context it's probably weeks and months. I wouldn't say we've reached a complete stalemate, that's all I know.

QUESTION: Perhaps you noticed or read the account in the Sunday New York Times Magazine on the buildup of Soviet warheads.

MR. GILPATRIC: Professor Jastrow's? Yes, I did.

QUESTION: Let's take his scenario as a hypothetical crisis situation. The Soviet Union might conceivably at some point announce that it would not allow any more satellites to fly over its territory and then shoot them down if they did. Let's take that scenario now and apply some of the rules for the Cuban missile crisis.

MR. GILPATRIC: Well, there are things we could do to counter that, of course. And I don't think that's an isolated kind of threat. They did shoot down U2s; Powers was shot down over the Soviet Union. And if they had the capability and if you have the kind of leadership in the Soviet Union that was prepared to take an extreme risk, I don't think that scenario of Jastrow's is too far-fetched. That's why I really shudder to think of getting into space wars. We have problems enough with verification in dealing with things that grew out of World War II, but when you get into lasers--I'm not enough of a scientist even to describe some of the concepts that are going through the engineering labs. I tell you, we've got an inventive group of engineers in this area.

THE PRESIDENT: ORGANIZING APPROACHES TO THE WORLD ECONOMY

Philip Klutznick

NARRATOR: We welcome Philip Klutznick and our guests to another Miller Center Forum. Partly because our guest feels so strongly about his relationships and his interaction with young people, we've gone beyond the traditions of the Forums in the past in that there are several excellent undergraduates with us. Secretary Klutznick particularly enjoys that relationship. As one of my colleagues said, "You won't need to introduce Phil Klutznick." He also said when somebody was preparing a list of visitors to come to talk to the political science department, "You've got the best list you could have right there with Phil Klutznick starting out the discussion."

Philip Klutznick was born in Kansas City. He was a student at the University of Kansas and the University of Nebraska. He received his law degree from Creighton University. He has a number of honorary degrees. He held public office in the 1940's as the director of the Federal Public Housing Agency. He was vice chairman of CED (Committee for Economic Development) and was one of the founding idea men that brought that important organization into being. He was a member of the delegation to the United Nations for the United States in the late 1950's and early 1960's. He was U.S. representative with rank of ambassador to the Economic and Social Council. He has continued to play a very central role in the refugee field, being a member of the Presidents' Advisory Committee on Indo-Chinese refugees. And he was, as many of you know, secretary of commerce in the Carter administration.

None of these things compares in my experience with the one in which I worked closely with him at an earlier stage. We both were associated with something called the Council on Religion and International Affairs that had been established by Andrew Carnegie, funded by Andrew Carnegie at the turn of the century. This was an interfaith group, but most of us wore our faith on our sleeve. The only person who really practiced this interfaith philosophy constantly and continuously, I thought, was Phil Klutznick and it was an inspiration to work with him at that time. So for that and for many, many other reasons--not least of the fact that it seems to many of us we sometimes neglect the economic dimension of the presidency and international economy--it's a great pleasure to introduce Secretary Philip Klutznick to speak on the presidency and the world economy and other subjects that suggest themselves to him and to you as he proceeds.

MR. KLUTZNICK: Thank you. I am overwhelmed by listening to my premature obituary. I am not really that good. I must tell you a secret. These have been busy days for some of us who get involved in international affairs in certain areas, so I didn't get down to preparing what I wanted to say here until the other day. I have a habit of coming in early in the morning and dictating what I want to say on a machine. I didn't get a chance to read it until I was on the plane this morning. And I tell you I didn't like it. It didn't impress me a whit. And so I said: "What am I getting into here?" The presidency and the world economy, it's an awesome subject to start with. I've found frequently in government that they have no relationship with each other but that's another subject. So I went through a lot of papers I had and I made some notes. When I got through I noticed that I was quoting myself. This reminds me of what is related to be an actual fact that the religious philosopher, Dr. Martin Buber, once said on that subject that there are really two stages in a man's life. The first is when he quotes someone else and usually it's from the gospel and he refers to the deity. And then the second stage is when he starts quoting himself. So a friend of mine who heard this statement said there's a third stage and that's when he mixes up the two. I hope that you won't consider some of the things that I'm about to say an effort to speak from on high, because I don't think that anyone who speaks about the state of the world economy and the President's relationship to it all, or the relationship of the presidency to it, can be too positive about either at this moment.

First of all, let us talk about the world economy from my perspective, at least. In the CED over a period of years we tried to make a modest contribution to sanity in that area. Some thought we were insane and sometimes we were really right, in retrospection at least. The economy itself is something that most people don't know how to define in terms of reality. It's amorphous. Economists are the only ones who really know how to define it and I know I'll be forgiven if I say that they're not always right. That's a modest statement, too. But if there's one thing that we can observe, that I think we can stand on in this discussion, it is that whatever the economy is or was, it has changed materially in terms of the world and our relationship to it in the last generation.

Let me go back a little beyond that. Ken has made reference to the time that I was in the UN. I recall full well when World War II ended and we were trying to decide what the financial assessment should be in the UN against the United States. Senator Vandenberg was then our representative on that committee and he was a man of extraordinary vision. Everyone contended that under the formula that had been developed, namely that a nation should pay in accordance with its share of the world gross national product, figures would show that we should have paid fifty percent. But, since Senator Vandenberg understood the UN better than some of the others, he said that would be a mistake. For any nation, one nation, to be responsible for half of the obligation would make the UN a kept woman. And therefore he finally argued them down to thirty-two plus percent. But the fact of the matter is that when World War II ended some figures will show that because of the devastation in the world we were at about fifty percent of the gross world product. And in manufactured goods some contend we were as close as seventy percent.

That's understandable. But where are we now and what's happened in between? I guess it's fair to say that we're still, with all of the recession around us, something under a quarter of the world's gross national product. Even during the miserable days when the national political campaign was on, we were over three trillion dollars in our gross national product which was maybe twenty-three percent--one nation of two hundred and twenty-six million people at that time out of four billion plus in the world. That sounds very impressive, but the fact of the matter is that if you look under the overall figures it's very depressing. Because in the things that really count into the future, we have been pretty much on the declining scale. The one bright exception, and how long that will continue no one knows, is agriculture, where we've demonstrated to the world that we can feed a good part of it with an ever declining manpower quotient. As a matter of fact at times it becomes a problem, internationally and otherwise, because of our food surplus, which we have this year again.

When it comes to manufactured goods, however, we're in a highly competitive area. I don't have to give you the newspaper reports of what's happened in terms of Japanese progress. What's under that report may even be worse in terms of our competitive position. MITI, the Ministry of International Trade and Industry, published an open report in 1980. We translated it into English and I was surprised to find how few people ever read it. In it they said candidly that up to now they had borrowed the technology of almost every advanced nation in the world and what they did was to improve on its development and use. And what an improvement they made. When we talk about robots, where did robots come from? Here. We just didn't develop them soon or in depth. Many ideas, especially in the electronic field, they borrowed from us. Perfectly legitimate, open competition. But then they added that the time has come when they have to do something more. They have to become creative. And Japan set aside over two billion dollars for the development of a science city at a time when they were already ahead of us in certain things. At the time they were doing that we couldn't get fifty million dollars out of the Congress for experimental applied research. This country does a wonderful job in supporting pure research and basic research and research related to military endeavor. But we have not been very long in letting the government get involved in matters that might have practical effects. The last report that I

17

read from Japan, supported by some evidence in this country, is that they have turned now to the computer industry to compete with us or our great producer IBM--not on hardware components but at the manpower component, the programmers without which the hardware is not very valuable.

If we could stop there it wouldn't be too bad. But what else has happened since the time we produced fifty percent of the world's gross national product? We now have added more than one hundred new nation states since that time. And Norman Cousins says with respect to matters of military endeavor, that the nation-state is of course the most useful instrument for the people because they can create more fury in an organized fashion that way than in any other fashion. We have among those hundred nation-states some new competitors. I didn't think some years ago when I visited Singapore that it might be becoming a competitor in many areas of manufacture and distribution of the United States. And when I bought my suits in Hong Kong I didn't fully appreciate what was happening in that little country. I won't even talk about Taiwan, South Korea, or even, in eastern Europe, East Germany, Poland, and Hungary. We are living in a highly competitive world in comparison with the late 1940's and the early 1950's.

I'm not sure we understand or appreciate what all this means. I'm not trying to be negative or partisan in what I'm about to say, because I don't see any evidence now of any change since we left office. There's been a feeling that the only way our free enterprise economy can be competitive is to free it completely. Take the government off our backs. Well, Ken has talked about interfaith--let me give you something from my faith. There's an old saying that goes back many years: "Pray for the stability of the government or else man will tear man apart." There cannot be freedom in the world, a free society where you don't have responsible government. There is a role for government. It is not to be on the backs of people, it is rather to help conciliate and to help cooperate with those parts of a society that are so essential to providing the things that our people need and other people need.

We were experimenting with this approach in the last years of the Carter administration. We experimented with it in steel and started to in automobiles in which we had the government at the cabinet level involved with the producers, the industry, and labor. And we managed to work things out, for which others are now claiming credit. We managed to come to a mutual understanding about a lot of things.

Let me cite an example. The first thing we did was to set up task forces to cover certain areas. There was so much complaint about how onerous the environmental regulations were and the industry

18

was getting nowhere in making its case. We studied it impartially and together. They had a proper complaint. It was not a complaint against the objective. No one can complain against getting clean air and clean water. Even an entrepreneur who is suffering from it finds it difficult to complain against it. But he can complain that his company cannot afford to do what has to be done to bring it about. And that was a just complaint. They couldn't do in the time allotted what the government law required, with the anticipated cash flow from the steel business. The solutions were very logical: extend the time. Don't change the objective. Make it possible or, in the alternative, help pay for it. And since we weren't going to help pay for it, one of the last things that Jimmy Carter did was to recommend a three year extension. And it was justified, completely justified.

The second thing we went to was technology. We had a sub-committee on technology. We live under a kind of an illusion that our job is to catch up with our competition. Anyone who has been in business long enough knows that by the time you catch up, your competition is ahead of you. So the assignment we gave to our technology committee was: how do we leap frog. And believe it or not the industry, labor, and the government agreed that the next technology was going to be to make steel like you make chemicals under a roof, in a continuous operation. You get away from all the environmental problems that are involved and on top of it you produce it at less cost than even the Japanese, who have become the standard for the most efficient operation.

When we agreed that that was the right thing to do we asked how much would it cost to produce one plant like that. This gives you an example of the kind of problem you run into. We all agreed it would cost a minimum of seven hundred and fifty million dollars to produce that plant. The technology was all there except for one or two things that they felt could be handled. But if you took a look at the financial statements of the biggest steel companies of America they couldn't afford to take that risk. It was going to take several years and it could be that at the end of the run it might not be as successful as all the estimates indicated. It was a logical proposition for government/business cooperation to do the technology, produce the result, and then turn it over to the private sector where it belonged for operation. And that was a program that we had recommended but it never got to Congress because time ran out for our administration.

It is problems like this that require the collective interest of the society and not just alone the industry. I believe with all my heart there are some things that free enterprise can't do by itself. So take that as one example.

19

Let me give you another one. This country has had the largest free market in the world. As a result everybody's come to us and sold to us. On the other hand, with all of our ingenuity and our ability, aside from the big companies that could afford it, small and medium-size businesses were not exporting in keeping with their strength. As a result, even though we maintained a surplus in current account which included everything, in exports we were running a deficit right along. In a large measure this was attributable to our import of energy. On current account we were constantly in surplus. Current account includes services as well as manufactured goods and products. And for a long while now (how long it will last I don't know) we have had an enormous surplus in our export of services whether it is computer service, lawyers, or architects. And on current account we were saved.

The Congress was alert to this problem. There must have been at least nine bills to help create export trading companies. If others copy from us there's no reason why we shouldn't copy from them as well. Japan's great success is due in part to its unique type of trading company. Those bills were laying around when I became secretary of commerce. By accident the chairman of the subcommittee in the Senate was one of my senators. He called me up one day shortly after I took office and said, "Look, I'm calling this bill up for hearing. It has been laying around for too long and you people have got to come up here so we can start creating export trading companies." I said, "Adlai, take it easy. I've only been here long enough to get my feet under the desk. All my reports are that everybody in the government is against it except you and a few senators. Give me a few weeks to work on it."

We worked on it. What were the problems? Again, this points up one of the problems as far as the world economy is concerned. You see it today in a minor way in connection with the Russian pipeline case--our antitrust laws. I don't make a case for all the people who think they ought to be kicked out the window. On the other hand, I get a little sick of those who have made of it an ideology or a religion. I was trained as a lawyer and I believe in what Brandeis used to say: "Law must follow social development. It cannot stay away from social and economic development." One of the most important cases I ever handled in the Supreme Court of my home state of Nebraska used the Brandeis briefing technique in order to get that conservative Supreme Court to approve public housing in the state of Nebraska.

We could not have an export trading company where eight or ten companies got together and were ready to have a joint venture because it could violate antitrust laws in one way or another. Not only that, these ventures cannot succeed too well, if there are small companies involved, without the love and affection of the banking system. And the federal reserve and the controller of currency said, "Look, they can borrow from them, but the banks can't invest in them." We had long hours in which I pointed to the fact that our banks had established themselves in foreign countries all over the world. They had branches all over the world. They were the best source for business. Yet these people were saying the banks couldn't even take a ten or fifteen percent interest in a small trading company in order that we might get competitive? We finally worked it out, except for House action, then the Congress adjourned. Maybe this month or next it will be enacted. With this power we will put to work the strongest force that this economy has, the small and medium-sized businessman, a sector that has added more employees to the economy than any other.

Therefore, all of these barriers which are in place created of necessity a situation where our influence in the nation's and the world's economy was declining. But there is another factor we cannot escape. The markets in the world are changing enormously. The Third World is a hope of the future for industrial countries if they develop those markets. Those markets can only be developed if we make it possible by the right kind of public assistance, multilaterally or bilaterally, for those countries to create the income levels where they can afford to pay for the products they buy.

In 1961 President Kennedy came to the United Nations and made his maiden speech before that body. And in one paragraph he called for a United Nations development decade to assist these countries to get into a position where they can be a competitive part of the society and produce their own wealth and be able to trade normally with other nations. At that time I represented the United States in the Economic and Social Council. It took me an hour and ten minutes to explain to the Second Committee of the General Assembly what the President meant in that one paragraph. And later on it took the Russians two hours to tell the world why that shouldn't be the objective. The objective should be to get rid of colonialism. But after we had negotiated a hundred and seven amendments we finally got a unanimous vote. At that time the United States was the number one contributor to these programs. I only looked at the OECD record the other day. Out of seventeen industrialized nations we rank thirteen. The goal was to be one percent of the gross national product in aid. The Netherlands was first with .99 percent. They didn't even quite make it. And we were thirteen with .27 percent.

The ability of the United States to influence the world economy is great. But not if our people don't understand what the world economy is all about and what is happening now.

I think it was Mr. Jefferson who said, "I'd rather not talk about the past, I'd rather talk about the dreams for the future." The past

I've spoken about. Where are we going now? We have a declining share of the world's gross product. If we don't learn how to trade, if we don't restore our relationship with the Third World, which is rapidly becoming an important influence in buying and otherwise, the only result we can look for is a rather dreary imbalance and a lessening impact on the world economy.

Let us talk about the presidency in that connection. Someone asked me--can the President do something about it? On occasion I've had my doubts, because Presidents in my experience are usually crisis managers. They find themselves in a position where foreign policy, security, or another emergency take most of their energy and time. But I've noticed in this administration a President can make a lot of difference in the economy. Ronald Reagan has kept some of his 1980 economic campaign pledges--I wish he hadn't. And he did it by the power of the presidency. As a result, we've got the largest rate of unemployment we've had since World War II. We have the largest deficit we've ever known in our history. We have the largest tax cut and the largest single increase in taxes in an election year all at once because the President wanted it.

Without his influence that combination of adversities--as I call them, and some people think that in the next year or two they'll pay off, maybe they will, I hope that they do--would not have been possible. We also have the largest defense budget in peacetime. I dealt with the Defense Department intimately on a number of occasions. The sensible generals and secretaries have always said one of the strongest parts of our defense is our home front. If we needed proof we got it in World War I--we got it again in World War II. And if we can't keep our economy going and we can't keep our competitive position up and we can't keep our people employed, we have weakened the very things that we're fighting for.

I noticed the other day that a task force in Congress introduced a bill to alleviate certain present conditions that would cost forty or forty-five billion dollars in the first year. I am not certain that the specific program should or should not be done. But when I relate that expenditure to increases in defense costs it represents about fifty or so of some of the more expensive aircraft that we're going to produce as projected now. What I'm trying to say as modestly as I know how, is that the presidency has to concern itself as much with our economic relationships to the world as it does to the security. No nation that is declining in its economic relationship to the competitive forces in the world can for long maintain the strength that it needs to be a world power.

This is the introduction to whatever questions you want to ask except for one other point. Our government has changed very much since my first service in the forties. During the war when I headed the agency that was in charge of the public war housing program, an incident arose which illustrates my view. The day after I took office I had to testify before the House committee concerned with the program. I had spent the whole night boning up on all the figures I could get. I got into the car to go to the Hill when the comptroller ran out and stopped the car. He said, "Mr. Commissioner, I'm afraid some of those figures are wrong." I said, "Herb, how could this be? I worked them over all night." He said, "Well, I have to tell you, we were an agency that was never concerned with war pressures. Under the war pressures we have not been able to keep our administrative work up to our production." "Well, why not?" He said, "Because there's a freeze on manpower and I can't get enough bookkeepers." I said, "Get into this car and come on up to the Hill with me. I'm not going alone!" The chairman of that committee was Tex Ranham. I said, "I've got to see you, Mr. Chairman, before we go in. We may be together a long while and I want you to know that we made some mistakes before we go out to that hearing." I told him the story. Once you get by with a thing like that I practiced it all the time thereafter. When I went before a committee, if I knew there was something wrong, I'd tell it to them before they caught me up with it. And there is always something wrong with the operations of an agency.

After the hearing I literally ran to the Bureau of the Budget. We only had a Bureau of the Budget at that time. I was able to see the director, Harold Smith, and I said, "Look, Mr. Smith, I'm in deep trouble." "What's the matter?" And I told him the story. He said, "How many bookkeepers do you need? I said, "Fifty." He said, "You've got them."

Even in those days during the war it was possible to get that kind of action. Try and do it today. The government has gotten so big. First, it would be undignified for the secretary to go over and see the GS12 who is handling our business. So someone else goes over. Then it goes through three layers, and by the time it's all over with, the cat's out of the bag and you've lost what you could gain. Fact is, those fifty bookkeepers, among other things, found that we were being stolen blind in some of our feeding operations. Meat was a scarcity in those days. Meat was coming in the back door of our cafeterias and going out the front door without ever having seen any heat and there were about eight or ten people who had to pay a penalty. At least we balanced our budget on feeding as a result of the fifty. Our government is so complex today that that kind of thing could not happen. The President or his top officers don't have the time.

Secondly, I went through two budgets as secretary of commerce. What happens is that the President and his immediate staff set a goal. How much can be spent overall? They make an estimate and then

23

they tell you "this is it, now you fit into it." Frankly I would have thought it was a better way for the people who were operating the agencies and the President to have a lot of preliminary discussions before an objective is set. We are the kind of conglomerate in government today where the President, as Mr. Jefferson once said, needs a dispersion of some of this power among his top people. I could conceive that the time will come when the secretary of a department will be told "you've got four billion dollars, you tell us how it should be spent." We may have to change the present system. If the Department of Commerce had been told, we would have cut out some other things, instead of the hundred and fifty million that should have gone for technology, productivity and innovation. We might have managed. We were in touch with that area. We knew where our troubles were. We knew we had to help industry in certain positions. We knew we had to get into studies that would show us, not the economy generally, but the sectors of the economy that were not only weak now but potentially would become weak in two or three years.

Example: we're number one in aerospace. Aerospace is in the fight now. We knew it was going to be in the fight two and a half years ago. What did we do to protect ourselves? We nearly lost major business in the world over one quarter of one percent interest rates on the theory that the richest country in the world couldn't afford to meet competitive rates of other countries.

This is where we are and somebody somewhere is going to have to awaken the American people to the reality that the President is as important in his knowledge and commitment to the world economy and our impact on it, particularly now, as he is to defense, diplomatic matters, or foreign policy. And unless we do, unless we create the cooperative atmosphere which is possible and essential, I see no immediate relief from the decline in our relative position in the world economy.

NARRATOR: Who would like to ask the first question?

QUESTION: The difficulty with policy and particularly with international economic matters, and this was the subject on which you addressed us, is that these are singularly unsexy subjects both in capturing any kind of charismatic banner and in the terms of mastering them. Foreign exchange fluctuations, mechanics of the Euro-dollar market: these are things that are enormously complex. It is asking a great deal of any President, it seems to me, and I would like it to be so, that Presidents should master these concepts. But people who come through the political process as our Presidents do, somehow along the way they have not acquired the concepts and techniques and understandings of these very intricate concepts. It's simply not there. I can't think of any modern President who really understood these things, in contrast to say someone like Chancellor Schmidt who understands or Giscard who understood these concepts extremely well. One of the funniest sections of the Nixon-Watergate tapes, this would be of interest only to the Congress I suppose, was when Halderman was trying to explain to Nixon the impact of the devaluation of the pound on the U.S. economy. The Miller Center is here to study the office of the presidency, and I'm not quite sure how the President can get enough advice. He can get very capable advice. But in order to appreciate the advice he has to start with a basic understanding of something enormously complex. And how we can expect, let's say, Mr. Reagan to understand....

MR. KLUTZNICK: Well, I think you've missed the point, if I may suggest it. I don't expect any President to understand what you understand about it. If he did it would be a mistake. Take the Department of Commerce. I had forty different kinds of operations, from telecommunications to fisheries to technology to bureau standards to laboratory investigation. I'd be a fool if I tried to understand the technology in all this. I did go out and see them all just to be sure that they were there, nothing more.

I have said to you, however, in a kind of parental way, that maybe the time has come for what Mr. Jefferson said a long time ago, that the most effective government is decentralized government. What do I mean by that? I mean that I don't think any President can be an expert in all things but if he has eight, ten, or twelve department heads, and I would consolidate some departments instead of expanding them, and he parts with a fractopm of his power to that institution and that institution has the ability like MITI does in Japan in the ministry to go forward with programs within the range of the total commitment, I think you would get more effective government. What you get today is second-guessing before the first guess has to be made. It's a matter of distribution of resources, of manpower, and people.

I had that problem when I was a young fellow and was frightened to run a government agency of twenty-six thousand people. What I did was to get closer to the people. I had my staff meetings very regularly with the experts, then I met with those people who were responsible for really running the government. Just like in a business. In the Department of Commerce, which had over forty thousand employees, I had ten to fifteen people that I had to meet with at least once a week to make sure I knew what was going on. We had forty who were running divisions and operations that we also met with once a week. But every two months the four hundred who were really doing the day-to-day work I would report to and they would raise questions with me, so that I was informed and could feel the tremors that were going on through that agency to see where our weak spots were.

25

Our weak spots were clear almost in the third month. We were in trouble on technology, we were in trouble on productivity; we knew that you couldn't maintain a standard of living in this country unless our productivity improved. We also knew since they had transferred the trade program to us that we couldn't continue to operate with the equipment we had in this modern world unless we improved our exports. It was obvious. And I had the authority to go ahead with it, subject to the congressional interference which takes some time. And someday we're going to have to learn how to keep our division of power without destroying ourselves in the process. Maybe some of our experts can tell us how to do that. No, the President should be the head of the enterprise. It would be foolhardy to expect him to operate it from his office alone. But some Presidents have tried. And that's been one of the problems.

QUESTION: I don't pretend to understand the economy better than the next man, but I am a little bit puzzled by a couple implications of your argument about the international economy which suggest to me that you may have one or two principles that are on collision course. It may not be the case and I would be glad if you could clarify it for me. If I understand it correctly the way you've put it is that the American contribution to the world economy has declined considerably since the Second World War. That, I think, is an inevitable consequence of a policy that the American government adopted after the Second World War, that the country would set out to rebuild the economies of Europe and the world in general in order to create new markets and to produce the kind of world stability that would allow American business to flourish. It seems to me what's built into that process of stabilizing the world and helping international economies to grow in order to have new markets, what's built into that process inevitably is that you're creating new competitors and therefore you're bringing about a decline in the percentage of the American contribution to the world economy. I can't see how you can set about creating large new markets without creating new competitors. And if you create new competitors you're bound to reduce the American contribution to the world economy.

If you go ahead and follow that principle through to the next stage, which seems to me to do the same for the Third World now as was done for Europe after the war, why have them go through the same cycle again? If you really set about building up the economies in the Third World you might indeed use a larger consumer demand in the Third World. But you are again inevitably going to reduce the American contribution to the gross national product of the world because other countries would be producing more. If it is the case that you equate American power with the size of its contribution to the world's economy, is this policy inevitably going to reduce American power and should that be accepted?

MR. KLUTZNICK: First of all, I've made the classic mistake of using percentages in one respect and not absolutes. It's done to me all the time so you're justified in your argument. First of all, I don't think we can look more than a generation ahead if we can look that far. I don't place much importance in the drop from fifty percent to twenty-three if it were a solid drop. What I place a tremendous amount of importance on is the weakness of that twenty-three percent, the fact that we have lost ground in our technological development. Forget what the percentage is. The fact is that we've lost ground in productivity, though I was glad to see a slight improvement the other day. The fact is that we have too many people unemployed.

I have a few other things that stare me in the face constantly. I was in Oregon. The lumbermen wanted to talk. What did they want to talk about? Even when business comes back we can't ship our logs. The roadbeds, the infrastructure won't take it. When are they going to improve it? When are we going to get our ports improved in the Northwest so that we can ship to Japan? The other thing that's happened that time didn't permit us to enlarge upon is that we have coal that the world wants and we can't get it out of our ports. You try and get thirty million tons of additional shipping out of Portsmouth. You may not even be able to get anything out of there if there is any military activity. Or, what we tried to do in piddling amounts in Boston. Our infrastructure which we have neglected, our transport, our railroads, even if we improve our situation we won't be able to get it out. What I really want to say is that there are short-term solutions and long-term. I would like to see someone among the experts make a study of what would be the net effect of transferring from unemployment--you can't transfer old people but for things like road building and roadbed building there are a lot of people who are unemployed today who could do a substantial part of that job and some of the port work--of transferring those people to rebuilding our infrastructure at a nominal subsidized pay as against the cost of paying unemployment. A cost benefit study. If the economy picks up, ask some of the big producers. How can they sell? I had former Senator Gore come in to see me when I was still secretary of commerce. Consolidated Coal had thirty million tons of coal sold if they could ship it out of a port. This country has an unlimited amount of coal. The demand for it is growing, not declining. And yet we don't have the way for getting it delivered abroad in great quantities. The same is true with lumber. Japan had to make a deal with Russia under which they put up all the money for the cutting and got back the lumber.

But what I'm trying to say is when one uses percentages and absolutes interchangeably it is confusing. If ten percent of the total gross national product is six trillion dollars, I'd rather have that than twenty-three percent or one fourth of six trillion. We'll never be perfect in this and no one is contending it, no one who runs a business is ever perfect. They may claim they are but they never are. What we're saying is that out of over four billion people there's a market out there. Let's develop it--let's help develop it. They can't buy from us unless they make things themselves. We made a study with Greece, which had a terrible imbalance of payment with us and I had to say to them, quit sending us tomato paste. Let's figure out what you can make that we can afford to buy so that you can have our business. So they started to make shoes. They couldn't begin to compare with Italy. There is a need for collaboration in the world. You'll find outside of South Africa and a few other spots in Africa, an enormous African need. Here we have this situation today as far as automobile production is concerned--if Japan was at full production they would make a minimum of thirteen million automobiles a year with overtime. If we were at full production and had our lines operating we could do that much. And if Fiat and the rest of Europe is doing what they should, we'd end up with thirty-five million automobiles. Where are you going to sell them?

The point is in order to keep the economy healthy I think you need to do several things. One, you have to improve your own operations. That is the most important. Second thing, you do what any of the other businessman does, you help develop new markets. There are needs involved. Forget percentages. I'm glad you caught that so I could explain it.

QUESTION: I'm concerned with American productivity and in the past I've been reading in newspapers and the media various reports speaking of the brain drain from academia into industry. As a result, we do not have the teachers in academia today that will teach science. We do not have the equipment and laboratories with which we can experiment. Is anything being done in that field?

That's one question. The second question is, when you have projects in development why does it take so long with Americans to take a project from design into production? By the time you get it into production, you're behind the competitors again. Is there any way you can cut the time span between the idea and production?

MR. KLUTZNICK: Well, let us take the first one. You have put your finger on one of the toughest problems that this country faces. It touches at several places. First at the input end. Recent budget activity is going to reduce the number of students. Maybe we're losing a lot of geniuses, who knows. And you are completely right. We have to get an input of young people who go into technical work. We have a shortage of engineers now. We have a shortage of good technical people now. And if the defense program gets up to its real level of production, which would fortunately take a little while the way they operate, we will be in worse shape. So I think that with all due respect to the need to balance a budget, and I want to talk about balancing the budget soon (I don't think it is going to come in my lifetime but I would like to talk about it anyway) it is more important to maintain the infrastructure and the manpower resource in a fashion where it can be productive. And I have heard back in our part of the country a number of complaints from universities and others of the kind of talents that is being lost. Maybe it's temporary. I hope it is. The cost of education in this country is very high. But you put your finger on a very important deficiency and I know no other way than to approach the problem by encouraging young people to go, in a way we have to encourage them.

Maybe the corporations will have to put up the money if the government does not, because otherwise they may be out of business in terms of their technology and their advancement. And some of them are doing it, incidentally. So to a degree that is helpful

But there's another aspect of this problem. We have recently seen a study by two Harvard professors in the business school. We have financial problems, management problems that may be worse than even what you are talking about. I've seen it in my own business activity in dealing with certain people who lead public companies, where short-term profits are the only way for them to make any money. And short-term profits may mean deciining future capacity.

Let me give you a concrete example. When I asked the Bureau of Standards to tell me how we could improve productivity they showed me one example of a machine tool which is basic in manufacture whereby merely changing the power plant in that same tool the one man who operated it could improve his output by sixty percent. Now, if in that plant the head of the plant and some of his associates are due to retire in a few years and the cost of the introduction of those power plants would show a bad profit year and no bonus, the human impulse to go forward is not there. And this is also a consequence of the absence of what one might call real industrial management as against account managers. Some may not like to hear this, but the Harvard study shows what I indicated to Ken. U.S. Steel spent seven hundred million dollars to buy Marathon which didn't improve the productivity in the U.S. steel one iota, and reduced the capital that might have been available to do so. So basically the manpower component, both at the executive end and at the labor end, is handicapped and the input is being reduced.

That sounds sour. I mean it to, because there is nothing in our studies that showed that there was any determination to change that. And I see nothing in the government's program that attacks the problem of productivity. The notion that if you free up a little more money and that would be used for increasing productivity doesn't hold very well. During the last go round before the inflation started we had depreciation levels that were good. They related equitably to reproduction costs. Much of that money was not used for that purpose. And the choices that are made have not been helpful to the total economy. I wish I could say something else. In my business, the development business, we have two kinds of developers: those who take depreciation and pocket it, and those who take it and use some part or all to improve their property. I'm afraid that's been one of the problems in our production machinery.

As far as the span of time for production, I know it's longer than it is in the country that you come from (Israel). The pressures in your country are different. The people have a different relationship to the production process. In the main your production units are smaller and the relationship between top management that needs the result and the people who are woking on it is more intimate. In our complex industry the gap between those who want the result and those that have to produce the results is greater. I guess that is a management problem. That doesn't mean that in a huge organization that you will cut your time very much but there's always room for improvement. And that's why I've said the small and the medium-sized business in this country, which incidentally out of nine million jobs that were added in the four years of the Carter administration provided six million of them, may be the rescue avenue for the kind of thing you're talking about. They can convert something over night.

QUESTION: I want to return again to our subject of the President and the presidency although we often have trouble here trying to talk about the presidency and ending up really talking about the President. Let me talk about him. From what I hear in your remarks you don't seem to hold much hope that the current administration or its leader will be able to make the kind of innovation that you would like to see and suggest that perhaps the decentralized system which would give more authority to this cabinet members would bring those innovations about. But I'm not sure about that and I wanted to ask you your opinion. For years liberals in the United States suggested that we should establish diplomatic relations with China, and Democratic Presidents never dared to do it and then President Nixon came in and was in a political position where he could not be assailed for being soft on communism. I wonder if President Reagan is not in a similar position of political strength. Although much of what he has done seems to be aimed at the idea of a free economy and taking government off the backs of the people, I see this primarily as urging that the government no longer step in to ensure redistribution of income to people at the bottom of the social ladder. If the market fails to bring about a redistribution, the Reagan administration is not going to step in and do it. But the innovations that you're speaking of are a very different kind of government intervention, where there is market failure or management failure of the kind you speak of which has prevented business from moving forward to carry out institutional innovation that will increase productivity. I can see Reagan using the power of the presidency and talking about a new partnership of business and government to compete more effectively in the world market. Why can't he do that?

MR. KLUTZNICK: If I were his advisor I would urge him to do that. I think you're completely right in your premise that he could get by with it easier than Jimmy Carter could. And Jimmy Carter was beginning to get by with it. Actually, the only reason some have hope is that he's still got two years plus to go, and he's demonstrated an ability to change a little and he has changed a little very recently. But, I have seen no evidence of the acceptance of the principle of a business/government/labor partnership, which is basic to this achievement. And it's no contradiction of his philosophy. Quite the contrary. I don't think his philosophy will hold and he may have to do this in order to achieve that philosophy. There's nothing in any program that he has submitted that suggests he has changed yet. As a matter of fact almost everything's been eliminated that was pointing that way. We had a modest cooperative program in certain areas of limited technology. That's all we could afford with the budget we had. We were seeking, really, the development of the Gaithersburg campus into a modern cooperative business/government/labor generating laboratory of new productive ideas. Under the present procedures the estimate is made at the beginning of the budget process through the processes of the OBM and operating at the lower levels and then the President reaches his goal; by the time you get through with that process and you take an appeal to the President it is too late to make any major changes because you're already up against the gun of getting to the Congress. And it would have to shake up the whole of that budget. If that input would come at the beginning of the process, a President would have an opportunity either himself or by delegated authority to reschedule priorities, which at this stage in our country's economic history calls for looking at the capacity to increase our gross national product rather than to reduce taxes. Because if you increase the gross national product, whatever the tax is it becomes a smaller portion of the people's and I don't think I see that. I hope in light of your statement that you'd get it to the President or his advisors.

NARRATOR: Mr. Secretary, for all of us, the kind of discussion you've led in an area that is somewhat removed from the ordinary discourse here has helped us enormously. Those of you who have the time may want to continue the exchanges after the meeting. Some of you have commitments, however. I think the fact that people have remained at this table late in the day is the best testimony of how helpful you've been to us. Thank you so very much.

PRESIDENTS AND CIVIL RIGHTS:
PUBLIC PHILOSOPHY OR PRAGMATISM

Harry Ashmore

NARRATOR: We are privileged to have another leading figure in the field of civil rights, Harry Ashmore, as our guest this morning. He was born in Greenville, South Carolina, and did his undergraduate work at a school which also has educators as well as football, Clemson. He was a Nieman Fellow at Harvard, and has honorary degrees from Oberlin, Grinnell, and the University of Arkansas.

Not only was he born in Greenville but he began his journalistic career there as a reporter for the afternoon Piedmont. In 1954 he went to Charlotte, North Carolina as editor; in 1947 he joined the Arkansas Gazette as executive editor; and in 1957 he and the Gazette were the first double Pulitzer prize winners in history for distinguished service in the Little Rock school integration controversy. He also received the 1957 Sidney Hillman Award for this contribution. Prior to the 1954 Supreme Court decision terminating racial segregation in public education, he directed a task force of forty-five scholars in a trailblazing survey of biracial eduation in the United States for the Fund for the Advancement of Education.

In 1955-56 he served as personal assistant to Adlai Stevenson in the Democratic presidential campaign. He has been chairman of the Advisory Committee of the California Democratic party. He has been a correspondent for the New York Herald Tribune, a columnist for the Los Angeles Times syndicate, and editor-in-chief of Encyclopaedia Britannica. He is the author of seven books, including The Negro and the Schools, An Epitaph for Dixie, The Other Side of Jordan, The Man in the Middle, Mission to Hanoi, Fear in the Air, and Arkansas: A Bicentennial History. He is very much at home in academia, not only through the Nieman Fellowship; he also has been Senior Fellow in communications at Duke University and the first Howard Marsh Visiting Professor at the University of Michigan. Many of you know him as a Senior Fellow of the Center for the Study of Democratic Institutions in Santa Barbara, where he was the strong right arm of Robert Hutchins through most of the Center's history. He was on the Board of Directors from 1954, executive vice-president and then president from 1969 to 1974. It is a great honor to have Harry Ashmore with us.

MR. ASHMORE: Thank you very much, Ken. The recitation is flattering except that I'm increasingly conscious of the dates you recited. It sounds like ancient history--the identification of an extinct volcano.

But I am here to talk about a current book--one published by McGraw-Hill in the spring. I spent the summer flogging it, as they say. I've now done a hundred TV and radio talk shows on the subject of the book--which might be called "Civil Rights As I Saw Them," but is actually titled Hearts and Minds: The Anatomy of Racism From Roosevelt to Reagan. I hope this gives me license to try to bring up to date for you the presidential reaction to this subject across the last fifty years.

One way to gain a useful perspective on the development of civil rights across time is to see it particularly, and primarily, as a political phenomenon, as opposed to the enduring moral issue it certainly has proved to be. It had its beginning at Philadelphia when the Founders were unable to deal with the question of slavery and swept it under the rug. It reemerged as the primary issue in a conflict that will be recalled around here, I'm sure. The Civil War only changed the formal dimensions of slavery, replacing it with what continued to be, at a minimum, the second-class citizenship visited upon the black population.

This form of racial discrimination was considered until World War II, with some reason, to be a peculiarly southern abberation, a regional phenomenon. Blacks had been concentrated as slaves in the southern states and continued to live there on the land, most of them, with only a relatively small migration to the great cities of the North. But the demography was abruptly altered by two World Wars and their aftermath. Today, no one could conceivably regard racism as a unique regional problem. It is quite literally, as Gunner Myrdal titled it when he published his definitive study in the 1940s, An American Dilemma, and it remains a dilemma because the basic issue remains unresolved.

My approach, as evidenced in Hearts and Minds, has always been more pragmatic than moral. I can't conceive how there could be a moral defense for slavery or for enforced segregation. So I have to stipulate that all my ancestors, and, I guess, most of yours, were on the wrong side of the moral question. And that, of course is a fact that conditions attitudes toward civil rights, along with all the rest of our region's peculiar history.

As a political matter race relations proved to be an insoluble problem for political pragmatists. No one, of course, can say anything in this history-drenched place without quoting Mr. Jefferson. Fortunately your Founder said something on every pertinent subject, usually on all sides, at one time or another. So I have quoted in Hearts and Minds what seemed to me to be his definitive statement of the attitude of that considerable body of Southerners who recognized that slavery was a moral wrong but couldn't figure out what to do about it. The issue to Mr. Jefferson was how to rid the country of

34

its black population, or to redistribute it to the point where it would no longer seem to be--whether it was in fact or not--a threat to the white population.

By 1820, Mr. Jefferson was arguing against the fateful compromise that drew a line across the southern border of Missouri and extended it to all the new territories in his Louisiana Purchase providing that those to the north would be free and those to the south slave. In reference to slavery, he said: "There is not a man on earth who would sacrifice more than I would to relieve us of this heavy reproach in any practical way. The cession of that kind of property, for so it is misnamed, is a bagatelle which would not cost me a second's thought if in that way a general emancipation, and-- the italics are his--_expatriation_ could be effected, but as it is we have the wolf by the ears and we can neither hold him nor safely let him go. Justice is on one scale and self-preservation on the other."

I suspect it would be fair to say that, whether spoken in those terms or not, that fairly represents the attitude of virtually every President in the United States from that time forth. All of them, including Abraham Lincoln, the emancipator, tried as best they could to avoid dealing with the issue of slavery. It became, of course, the focus of the growing division between the North and South. It was condemned by the abolitionists of the non-South, and defended in the South on moral grounds, obviously without very much success. The southern rationalization was that the peculiar institution provided a means of converting a primitive people to Christianity, and thus introduce them to a somewhat limited version of the blessings of western civilization. There's no point in belaboring the old controversy except to say that in terms of politics it became and remained the dominant national issue in those formative years. I've often thought what a profound effect the mere presence of the black population, initially against its will, has had on all our basic political institutions, and still has. For example, after the Civil War and Reconstruction there emerged the one-party South; the purpose of that Democratic monolith was to disfranchise the blacks, but the result was to determine the ultimate shape of national politics for a hundred years.

Growing up in South Carolina between the world wars, I entered college in 1933, the first year in the New Deal, so my political consciousness began under Franklin Roosevelt. My native state, you will recall, was the first to secede, and I've never been sure it has rejoined. We were in those days totally, monolithically Democratic. A family joke had it that when I got to be sixteen years old, my father took me over the Blue Ridge to Tennessee to show me a Republican. Certainly I'd never seen one in Greenville.

Later, when I went down to, cover the state legislature for the Greenville News, I recall attending the state Republican Convention in the days when the party was headed by "Tieless Joe" Tolbert. As Republican state chairman he had no function except to name the postmasters when the GOP was in office, and in the Roosevelt years he and his followers were waiting in the desert. The faithful, including several blacks, convened in a small hall in Columbia. When the time came to elect the Republican State Committee, which required sixteen members, they named everybody present and still had one vacancy. One of the black Republicans arose and pointed over to me and said, "I don't know this young white friend over here, but he's got a good Republican face. I want to put him in nomination." The only speech I ever made in a Republican gathering was to prevent my election.

The fact was that race simply was not a political issue in the pre-World War II epoch of the New Deal. The blacks were totally disfranchised, had no vote, no political clout of their own. Some of the social changes taking place under Roosevelt's aegis benefited the poor generally, and the blacks of that day certainly qualified on that score, but there was no separate concern with the matter of segregation. There were many practical reasons why Mr. Roosevelt chose not to make an issue of it, including the fact that the senior members of the Congress, the powerful committee chairmen, were mostly southerners because of the long tenure the Democratic monolith provided for them. FDR's most resounding political defeat came when he attempted to purge obstructionist senior senators, and went into the Democratic primaries in the South and spoke against them. The list, as I recall, included Senator Byrd of Virginia, "Cotton Ed" Smith of South Carolina, and Walter George of Georgia, among the six he singled out. I heard him when he came to South Carolina to urge the citizens not to return Cotton Ed for his sixth term. I'm convinced that it was this "outside interference" that reelected Ed, who seemed certain to be defeated.

Every one of the southern Senators on Mr. Roosevelt's purge list was renominated in the Democratic primary, which was of course the election. What the President didn't recognize was the strain deep in the Southern consciousness which I managed to identify on television the other day, a breakthrough I'm very proud of, by pointing out to a CBS interviewer the southern syndrome epitomized by the saying, "Ain't no son of a bitch gonna tell me what to do." So when the President came down and told the voters what to do, the reaction was immediate even though most of them continued to vote for--and even idolize--Mr. Roosevelt.

But in World War II the race issue was drawn in a new and compelling fashion for a number of reasons, not the least of which was the resumption of the out-migration of blacks from the South which had begun during World War I, and then slowed in the depression years. Blacks were now concentrated in the inner cities of the

North--Chicago, Harlem, Boston, Philadelphia. There they could vote and so they acquired at least local leverage on the big city political bosses. On the moral front Eleanor Roosevelt took up the cause of the blacks in the South, insisting that segregation must end. She spoke out across the region and became a kind of a pariah to a great many whites.

I date the beginning of the civil rights movement as an essentially political phenomenon from the threat by A. Phillip Randolph, the head of the Pullman Porters Union, to lead a black march on Washington to protest Jim Crow segregation in the armed forces, which was total at that time and to demand the opening of jobs for blacks in the booming wartime industries. Roosevelt headed off the march by meeting with Randolph in the White House and offering compromises. He didn't end Jim Crow in the Army, that didn't come until Truman did it in 1948, but he did make concessions: he created some black combat units and he opened up the promotion of black officers. Prior to that time most blacks had been consigned to menial jobs in service units. That was a considerable concession, but even more important was the creation of the first Fair Employment Practices Commission, empowered to employ the leverage of the federal government to insist that any industry with a military or federal contract had to end discrimination in its work force. Since practically every industry in the country was under Federal contract at that time, this spurred the out-migration from the South. It marked the beginning of the great concentrations of black population on the West Coast--in Los Angeles, Oakland, the San Francisco Bay area. Blacks went out there because the shipyards and aircraft plants were there--and in need of manpower. And it also opened up a higher level of employment, generally speaking, for blacks than they had had access to before.

President Truman continued the wartime FEPC. and also ordered the desegregation of the Armed Services. The generals and the admirals dragged their feet for quite a while, but by the time of Korea, desegregation had begun and there were integrated units all the way down to squad level.

There were now purely political reasons why Mr. Truman began to move on the civil rights front. In 1948 Clark Clifford, his astute counsel, concluded that Truman's reelection depended upon his getting a substantial vote from white liberals in the North and the black vote, which by that time migration had made a significant factor in the Democratic strongholds of the North and West. So Mr. Truman created a Civil Rights Commission, a very high-powered one. The Commission came forth with the report that really set the agenda for what later became federal action, as the report was titled, "To Secure Those Rights." Much of this wouldn't take place for another twenty years, but the call for the end of discrimination in voting, public accommodations, employment and education would be heard in every succeeding national election. Truman sent up a package of civil rights legislation embodying some of his Commission's recommendations. This never got through Congress and nobody really thought it would. But it did split the Democratic Party, and 1948 became the year of the Dixiecrat Rebellion. Strom Thurmond of South Carolina and Fielding Wright of Mississippi ran on a rump States Rights Jeffersonian Democratic ticket, carried four southern states with 39 electoral votes. There was also a rebellion on the other flank, the Henry Wallace Progressive movement which split off on the left. The primary motivation for Wallace and his followers was to protest the cold war with the Soviet Union. But in order to dramatize his left perspective Wallace made a tour across the South in which he denounced any form of segregation, refused to stay in any facility that was segregated, and created quite a traveling circus as he came down across the Carolinas and wound up in Arkansas at Little Rock where I interviewed him on radio. I later had to interview Strom Thurmond to provide equal time.

From that time forward, civil rights became an absolutely inescapable issue for any Democrat who was running for national office, although it would not become a dominant issue until 1960 when Jack Kennedy made it one. In the interim, I spent 1956 with Adlai Stevenson in the wilderness. I signed on as a personal assistant during the nomination campaign because by then I could see what was coming. I'd done the study for the Ford Foundation that resulted in the book called The Negro and the Schools. Litigation before the Supreme Court had moved school desegregation to the top of the civil rights agenda, and now the Court had ordered the end of the dual school system in its historic Brown decision. There could be no doubt that such a massive change in social practices would create grave problems across the South.

My decision to join Adlai Stevenson's campaign entourage stemmed in large part from my conviction that the great failure of that critical period was that of President Eisenhower. When the Supreme Court handed down the Brown ruling in 1954 it deliberately built in a year's delay before any school district would be required to take action, setting a further hearing a year later to determine how to implement the decision. The Justices recognized that this was going to create a critical problem for the local school boards, city governments, and state governments that had to deal with it and across the South local leadership that would at least accept the necessity of making this change. And they clearly hoped that Mr. Eisenhower would use the great moral weight of the presidency to at least urge peaceful compliances. But Eisenhower refused to make a statement that went beyond the minimum declaration that he accepted the ruling of the Supreme Court as the law he was sworn to uphold.

There were some southern political leaders, particularly in the upper South, who spoke out in support of orderly compliance, including the Governor of Virginia--Stanley it was in those days. It wasn't exactly an endorsement but they did say, in effect, "We are going to obey the law, we're not going to have massive resistance, we're not going to have rioting." But in that year of grace, while Eisenhower remained silent, support for these leaders began to fade and massive resistance began to build across the South. White Citizens Councils came into being, pledged to use nonviolent means, but to resist to the last ditch. By the time the Court got around to issuing its implementing decrees the moderate voices in the South had fallen silent and Governor Stanley had reversed himself. The pattern then was clear; in the upper South there would be some gradual accommodation, with this real resistance coming in the deep South--South Carolina, Georgia, Alabama, Mississippi, Louisiana.

As nearly as I could trace Eisenhower's attitude, trying to follow it through the literature, I could only describe it in Hearts and Minds a kind of a petulant neutrality. He wanted the whole issue to go away, he had no sense, no feeling for it. He had been isolated from the real world through most of his adult life in the military, and he had opposed, as chief of staff, Truman's desegregation of the Armed Services.

This is speculation after the fact, but I've always believed the situation would have been different--the transition in the South much easier--had the President spoken up, had he made a direct appeal to the leadership of the South at least to uphold law and order. I think he could have brought out the Chamber of Commerce types, the conservative businessmen who did come forward later when they recognized that they simply couldn't afford the economic cost of racial disorder. When the South began to massively desegregate, it came about because the politicians had the support of the conservative business leadership.

I've said that the moderate governors who emerged all across the South, including Jimmy Carter and those of his political generation, did not produce the climate of moderation, but were produced by it. The citizenry, always ahead of the politicians on the issue, finally made it clear that it was willing to accept the change. We'd been through Little Rock where Orval Faubus invalidated the resistance strategy, the legal statutes that had been devised to provide "a generation of litigation"--he used them all up in one year. And Faubus also forced General Eisenhower to act when he seized Central High School with his own state militia. By calling out the National Guard he drew an issue Eisenhower couldn't avoid, so the President put on his general's hat and demonstrated that he had more troops than Faubus did; he sent in the 101st Airborne and the re-run of Fort Sumter was over that afternoon. Thereafter, the Little Rock case went three times to the Supreme Court, which unanimously knocked down all the resistance devices Faubus tried, including his effort to set up a private school system and use tax money to support it. This was, I think inevitable, for Faubus was attempting to rally support for a Deep South strategy that could not long command support in Arkansas, an Upper South state where the pattern should have been that of North Carolina and Tennessee, not that of Mississippi or Alabama.

In 1956 the situation cried out for a healer who could hold the Democratic party together and persuade its local leadership to accept a moderating role. Adlai Stevenson tried to assume that role, while Eisenhower--whose party had effectively written off the black vote since New Deal days--simply avoided any discussion of the civil rights question. Stevenson, of course, could not follow suit even if he had been disposed to. His efforts at conciliation led the black leadership to accuse him of trying to straddle, every time he'd make a law and order appeal, it would outrage the left liberals. Many of those who write about that period talk about Stevenson's waffling on civil rights. I don't think he did; it was simply that he couldn't establish a position satisfactory to either the diehards in the South, or the black leadership and their white supporters in the North. He was trapped in the middle, as every Democratic politician would be for another decade.

I've just come from Atlanta where I attended the annual meeting of the Southern Regional Council, where Hearts and Minds was honored with the Lillian Smith award. The occasion was a reminder of the irony that has always attended the civil rights movement, for Miss Lillian in her day denounced the Southern Regional Council as much too moderate for her. One night in early 1960 Miss Lillian went to dinner with Martin Luther King and his wife Coretta. They drove her back to Emory University Hospital, where she was being treated for cancer, and when thev crossed into Dekalb County, an old Klu Klux Klan stronghold, a policeman saw a white woman sitting on the front seat by a black man and automatically stopped the car. Then he discovered he had Martin Luther King, and that King still had an Alabama driver's license. So the young preacher was given a fine and a suspended six months jail sentence for failure to obtain a Georgia driver's license.

Some months later King led a student sit-in at Rich's Department Store and went to jail to dramatize his protest. Mayor Hartsfield had him sprung in twenty-four hours but the judge in Dekalb County decided King had violated his parole. So they hauled him back to Dekalb and whisked him off in the dark of night to state prison under a six months sentence. Coretta King was terribly upset, and called Harris Wofford, the civil rights adviser for John Kennedy, then coming into the home stretch of his presidential campaign. Kennedy called Mrs. King and reassured her that Bobby Kennedy had gotten in touch with the judge over in Dekalb and that her husband would be released. So Martin Luther King came back to the Ebenezer Baptist Church--old Daddy King's church--in triumph, with national TV cameras there to record the scene.

Daddy King had been supporting Richard Nixon on the ground that a Baptist preacher couldn't endorse a Catholic, but now he made a public announcement that since Mr. Kennedy had done this for his son he was switching his vote. And it is generally believed that this highly publicized conversion resulted in Kennedy's carrying black precincts all over the country by majorities that provided his narrow margin of victory. So the young President took office beholden to Martin Luther King, Jr., and became the first chief executive to commit himself to the use of federal authority to advance the civil rights movement.

There is a lovely story about Jack Kennedy's receipt of word of Daddy King's recantation of his anti-Catholic bias. "Who would have thought that Martin Luther King, Jr. would have a father who was a bigot?" Kennedy remarked. Then he paused a moment and said, "But, then we all have fathers."

As it turned out, Kennedy didn't have enough political clout to get the more significant measures he proposed through Congress. Nobody can know what might have happened without the assassination that brought Lyndon Johnson to the presidency.

But it can be said that Johnson had a feeling for the basic issue no President before him had. He'd lived with racial discrimination, he knew what it was about. And I think that, whatever else may be said about him, he must be reckoned as the one most responsible for the great sea change in race relations that has taken place in our time. He also was a great political manipulator who knew how to handle Congress. Using the great advantage of emotional response to the martyrdom of Jack Kennedy, he persuaded Congress to enact his civil rights package as a memorial to his slain predecessor.

The result was the Great Society program, as Johnson called it, the War on Poverty. We will never know what might have come of Johnson's dream had it ever been adequately financed and administered. As it came into being, the civil rights movement, which had been taken to the streets, gave rise to a student movement soon embroiled in anti-Vietnam War protest. King, true to his non-violent Gandhian precepts, was the only black leader to join the peace movement, and his split with Johnson effectively ended the civil rights movement as concentrated on issues of race. Still, the move ment left behind it a residue of legislation that produced a significant change in prevailing majority attitudes in the country. Affirmative action, as it came to be called, produced major social progress before Richard Nixon, and now Ronald Reagan, set out to reverse the direction of public policy.

In a single generation--twenty-five years is the span we are talking about, thirty at most--the black middle class has greatly expanded. Today about a third of the black population now would be classified as middle-class in terms of educational attainment, income, type of occupation, and lifestyle. And these blacks have been pretty much accepted as equals by the majority white middle class. While there remains a residue of racism and bigotry, we have dismantled institutional segregation, the upper strata of the black population has been able to move effectively into the mainstream.

Another third of blacks are classified by the sociologists as "working poor," still below the mid-level of income but in the work force and, generally speaking, upwardly mobile. These are the ones who have been hardest hit by the recession, under the law of the marketplace that provides that the last hired is the first fired.

The great, enduring problem is the so-called underclass, the third of the black population primarily concentrated in the great cities, most of them outside the South. They are in the third generation of welfare dependency, trapped by self-perpetuating poverty. In many cases they simply do not have the capacity to move into the work force if there were jobs for them. The family structure has virtually been destroyed by this experience, and certainly there is going to have to be some kind of government intervention, some forms of affirmative action, if we are to do more than simply sustain the socially unfit as welfare dependents. And this, as I see it, is the great problem that President Reagan refuses to face. It's not that I think he's racist; I don't even think that's relevant. The tragedy is that he has accepted the states' rights doctrine our forefathers perfected in defense of slavery, accepted it quite literally. He talks about a new federalism. But what he's offering is the old federalism, the federalism that permitted slavery and institutional segregation to flourish. I can't imagine that in the end it will work. His economic policies, of course, are hitting hardest at the poor, and the blacks are disproportionately among the poor. But, aside from the question of justice, he is ignoring not only the lessons of the bloodshot past but contemporary demography. The black underclass exists now at the very core of all our major cities. When you talk about the urban crisis, this is what you're talking about. You're talking about an unassimilated mass of people who have never gotten into the economic mainstream, and in many cases no longer have any capacity for upward movement. We have created surplus population, and now we are manufacturing criminals.

Mr. Reagan's successor is going to have to deal with this problem. And it's going to require a return to at least a basic proposition represented by the reforms that took place from the New Deal through the Fair Deal through the Great Society. The short-hand name for it is affirmative action. I don't think the old programs can simply be reinstated. But what we've got to get back to is the basic assumption that the federal government shares a direct responsibility for guaranteeing equality of opportunity for all of its citizens, wherever they may be. That is the concept Ronald Reagan has quite formally abandoned. He denies that the federal government has such responsibility; to the extent that government has an obligation to the disadvantaged it should be discharged at the local and state level, and in any case it can best be taken care of through the working of the private sector, that is, through a process of social Darwinism made possible by economic growth. I think he's wrong on all counts, and we've got another crisis coming.

NARRATOR: I think everybody would agree that for an extinct volcano, Harry has thrown out a lot of sparks, history, ideas, food for thought. Who'd like to ask the first question?

MR. ASHMORE: I warned you I was programmed by all those talk shows.

QUESTION: As a pragmatist, how do you see any candidate for national office putting together a coalition that would address this? Because as I've seen it here in Virginia for eighteen years, code words of racism have been in every election. And more often than not, at least here, we've lost.

MR. ASHMORE: Look at George Wallace--the resurrection of old George. The only way George could get back in office was to be a born-again integrationist, repentant of his race-baiting past and guaranteeing Alabama blacks that he's going to look after them, and so they voted for him.

QUESTION: Are you suggesting that we need to rely on the black population?

MR. ASHMORE: Well, I've just been talking to Claude Sitton, the editor of the News and Observer in Raleigh, who pointed out that in North Carolina Jesse Helms backed six congressmen and lost every one of them. Now this has to say something. An issue of the Atlanta Constitution I was reading on the plane yesterday had an election round-up indicating that moderates--I don't know what a moderate is these days but at least it's not Strom Thurmond and Jesse Helms--most of the moderates seemed to have returned to office all across the South under the Democratic banner. That seemed to be the reading that most people are putting on the election returns. Roy Reed, who covered the South during the troubles for the New York Times is now teaching at the University of Arkansas and has the greatest dateline of any journalist I know--Hog Eye, Arkansas. He wrote a piece for the Arkansas Gazette which made this point about Wallace: the great irony is that George Wallace has done what Martin

Luther King tried to do and failed to do, that is to create a populist coalition of redneck whites and blacks. That coalition may not hold but that's exactly what he put together in Alabama. And I think that's going to say something for the future.

We're in retrograde on the school question, there's no doubt about that. We are resegregating primarily because of demographic change plus white flight. But on almost every other front there is a very significant change. We've desegregated public accommodations, and we're not going back on that. I'd say Atlanta is the most desegregated city in the United States today. And of course in the major cities you are getting black city government--you have one there headed by Andy Young.

So far, Reagan has reconferred the whole black vote on the Democrats, and because of the way it is concentrated that's a substantial political asset. The pollsters in California are trying to figure out the effect of race prejudice on Tom Bradley, the black Democrat who almost got elected governor but didn't quite make it. The one who runs the Los Angeles Times poll figured that there was about a two percent net anti-black bias vote, and the election was so close that that probably accounted for the election of Dukmejian over Bradley. The analysis was made on the basis of exit polling--the number of people who said they thought blacks were getting excessive amounts of government attention, that was the key test question-- being larger than the number of whites who said they thought blacks needed more attention. That was the bias test, and it seems awfully loose to me.

If we want to be optimistic you could say the most significant thing about California is that Bradley has been elected mayor three times in Los Angeles, the second biggest city in the country, and was almost elected governor--and that all but less than twenty percent of his supporters are whites. That could not have happened twenty-five years ago, even twenty years ago.

The real problem is more deeply affected by economic considerations than by racial attitudes--that is, how do we mobilize resources to begin to deal with the black underclass? My own view is that we will have to rely on the educational system. We've got to think about getting to these underclass children in the preschool years, because if they come to the first grade or kindergarden without basic communication skills and motivation, they're never going to make it in the public school system. There's no way that they can participate in group instruction. Now, how you do that is another question.

I'd say the most dangerous thing that Reagan is proposing is a tax exemption for private school tuition. If that should be put through I think it would virtually finish off the public school system, which is already in bad enough shape. It's a disaster area in almost every city for a variety of reasons, not just the desegregation question. We have always depended on public education as an ultimate social panacea in this country, the means of solving the acculturation problems posed by "the melting pot." To turn away from it at this juncture would seem to me to be a grave, if not fatal mistake. Now, what the prospects are for doing tuition tax exemption, I don't know. Certainly as far as the Reaganomics school of thought is concerned it is a basic commitment, and I suppose they will continue to work on it.

QUESTION: Let us go back to this matter of electing blacks to official positions. Do you see the possibility of a kind of phasing, that the blacks can win at the local level but not the state level, and why is it we have, I think, no blacks from the South in the House of Representatives? Isn't that correct?

MR. ASHMORE: Well, they didn't replace Andy Young, but there are a couple of black members of Congress from other southern states. That's a problem of course. But on the other hand, in North Carolina they doubled the number of blacks in the legislature. Of course, the obvious problem is if the voting is on the straight race basis, on a self-interest basis, there is no place where the blacks will have a state-wide majority. The only majorities they have are concentrated mainly in the urban places, where they increasingly are taking over City Hall.

It is going to be a problem and there are a series of legal actions going on involving redistricting and voting at large, and these are still in the courts. It is an unsettled area. The effort to keep black representation down, principally at the municipal level, has been to go, where it's appropriate, to a city-wide vote, or where it is inappropriate to go to a ward vote so you can do a lot of juggling and redistricting.

I think the most significant case--and I was surprised that the Supreme Court announced last week that they are going to rule on it-- is the one coming from Boston which involves affirmative action in the most direct way. A federal court there has ordered the police and fire departments to desegregate under a quota, until employment reflects the percentage of black population. They had begun to get close to that, but they've also got a state law which requires that in case of a reduction of force, seniority must apply. Then they had a Proposition 13 style tax cut and the Boston police and fire departments have had to cut back about twenty percent, so everybody who was being laid off was black. They are claiming that they are required to lay off the last-hired under the civil service seniority regulations.

45

The Supreme Court has agreed to take those cases and that is certainly going to pose the affirmative action quota question in a way that's inescapable because it is a qualitative, demonstrable proposition. You don't have to argue about motivation. How this Court will go on that I don't know; they conceivably can rule that the civil service seniority regulation should prevail. If that happens, it would be a nearly mortal blow for many desegregation employment programs. It would probably affect women about as much as it would blacks because there is a similar issue involving them. The seniority question is very real to them because they also are late-comers in many areas of unemployment.

QUESTION: I want to ask a question, particularly since you say Reagan is now delivering the black vote back to the Democratic party. Is there any likelihood in your judgment of a southerner being elected President again in this century?

MR. ASHMORE: I think it's going to be difficult. Of course these things could change very rapidly. I would think that attitudinally the country seems to be quite fluid--flowing in the wrong direction, in my view, usually--and must be suffering some kind of national schizophrenia when the polls show that Reagan continues to be popular although the people who like him oppose everything he's doing. This seems to be the fact all across the country. He is a great communicator, I suppose that's a part of it, but it seems to be more than that.

I don't see any enduring reason why we can't have another southern President. The patterns here in the South are no longer significantly different from those in the country at large, economically and politically. But I must admit that the old South that I buried in the book called <u>An Epitaph to Dixie</u> still exists as a metaphor. I guess it's partly nostalgia, but I feel more southern every day for some reason. Maybe it's because I'm no longer living here, which might make it easier. I don't know, I think it is a transition time and I think we are going to see, for better or worse, further institutional changes.

What we're seeing now in terms of economic dislocation is not going to be cured by a resumption of growth or getting a Keynesian economist back in power. A lot of this unemployment is structural, a result of technological change, and we simply have not caught up with it. We don't really yet appreciate the fact that we have automated agriculture in this country to the point where there is practically no population left on the farm. There was no anticipation of what the result of this has turned out to be in the case of the displaced blacks who have wound up in Harlem and Philadelphia and Chicago and Los Angeles. That's where they came from. Some were leaving the South because of discrimination, but most were leaving because there was no longer a job for them on the land.

That's not a very satisfactory answer, some people say we're going back to the one party South as a result of the recent midterm election. I doubt that. In fact I don't think the party labels mean much any more. You've got factions within the Democratic party, whatever they're called, which range from conservative to liberal, with moderates in the middle.

The most alarming story I read yesterday in the Constitution was a lead story on page one quoting local agricultural experts who say that if the present trend continues--Georgia is still about sixty percent agricultural in terms of income--if the present trend continues in the next twelve months thirty to fifty percent of the farming operations will fail. The implication of this for the banking system of course is enormous; practically all of the banks, if they called in their farm mortgages, would be bankrupt. And this is true in every agricultural state across the union, including the Midwest. So that could be the beginning of a real depression, as it was once before.

QUESTION: You made the point that many people have made that President Johnson was able to use the Kennedy assassination as one major way of motivating the passage of civil rights legislation in 1964 and thereafter. Could you have seen a comparable movement in civil rights legislation had it not been for the Kennedy assassination?

MR. ASHMORE: I think not. I think it would have come but it would have come later and it wouldn't have come in the dramatic and rapid way that it did. In the book I recall, about two weeks before the assassination in Dallas, having lunch with Scotty Reston of the New York Times in Washington and he was talking about the fact that Kennedy's whole program was absolutely on the rocks. He wasn't getting anything through Congress, and furthermore Reston doubted that he could be reelected. Kennedy was far down in the polls. We tend to forget this because the record was wiped out by the high drama of Dallas. But I think that indicates that it would have been very unlikely that Kennedy could have gotten the civil rights package through.

QUESTION: Do you see this in any way an indication, not just that Kennedy was less successful than Johnson in manipulating Congress, but that maybe Kennedy's civil rights legislation wasn't quite as strong as Johnson's?

MR. ASHMORE: Well, I don't think that Kennedy had the deep feeling for it that Johnson had. Jack Kennedy was, after all, the product of his background. He thought about discrimination as being wrong, as people at Harvard had always thought it was wrong. But until he became President he accepted it as a fact of political life--it wasn't fair, but then, he said, life's unfair. So I don't think he had that gut impulse. I think he was prodded into action by circumstances, and in part, as I suggested, by the obligation he owed Martin Luther King. And of course, by that time we had entered the period of demonstrations, the street marches, and he, like Eisenhower, had to restore order. When Bull Connor called out the dogs and the firemen and turned on the fire hoses in Birmingham, he couldn't tolerate that.

Incidentally, there is another wonderful anecdote about Kennedy that comes from Coretta King's memoir, I think. When Martin Luther King and his assistants went to Washington after they'd won in Birmingham and the "white only" signs had come down, they met with Kennedy in the White House and he said, with his usual irony, "You know, you all shouldn't be too hard on Bull Connor. He may have done more to advance civil rights than anybody since Abraham Lincoln."

Now Bobby Kennedy--I've never understood Bobby, I don't think Bobby ever saw the world the same way I did. He had what amounted to a death-bed conversion after the assassination. He had had very little interest in the civil rights issue in his early years. He began to, I think on a pragmatic basis, when he was attorney general because he could see the political advantages. But, when he was a lawyer on John McClellan's committee staff, he seemed to be about as much a white supremacist as anybody on the Hill, insofar as his work indicated. He was obviously deeply affected by the assassination of his brother, and when he ran for President himself it was almost as though he was on a crusade for all the downtrodden--the Indians, the blacks, the Chicanos. I don't doubt his sincerity, but again we will never know what he might have done because there was a tragic end to his story too.

QUESTION: Have you extended your interest to the problems of the Chicanos, and the illegal immigraion, and all that sort of thing?

MR. ASHMORE: Well, although I live in the shadow of it, I can't say that I have. In the book I tried to stick with the thing I've been stuck with, which was the race problem. But it's a complicating factor and in California it's dramatic. The projections now are that they will be the majority--the Chicanos--statewide by the end of the century. And there are significant differences. There is probably more tension between blacks and Chicanos than there is between blacks and whites. In Los Angeles for the first time since World War II we are seeing teen-age gang warfare, fighting for turf, and it's almost always a Chicano gang versus a black gang.

The Chicanos have their separate culture and language and this poses a distinctly different problem from that posed by blacks. Although the leadership will say they want to desegregate, their real

48

desire is to maintain separate schools where children can be taught in Spanish. However, the cultural unity produced by allegiance to the Catholic church seems to be diminishing. A great many Chicanos have been converted by store-front evangelical Protestants. The Church doesn't seem to have the enduring hold on Chicano immigrants that it had a generation ago, and that seems to be changing the family pattern. They are subject to the forms of family destruction that afflict poor blacks. And now we've got a large and growing Asian population in California from the backwash, from the southeast Asian war--Vietnamese, Laotians, Cambodians plus a large Korean community. That complicates matters too. And finally, the extension of affirmative action programs to women has created additional competition for scarce jobs once reserved for minority males. All these conflicts are inevitably accentuated by a shrinking economy. When things were expanding you could make social changes without actually taking anything away from anybody because there were new positions to fill, but when two people are competing for one job, whoever loses is going to believe he was discriminated against if the winner was another color or sex.

QUESTION: You mentioned the Kennedys, with one notable exception, and mentioned other candidates. I wonder if you'd care to assess the potential of the current Democratic possibilities for addressing constructively some of the issues you've discussed this morning.

MR. ASHMORE: Well, I would take any Democrat, and I like Ted Kennedy. But I don't believe he's going to make it in the end, although the Washington Post had a think piece this morning saying that the Kennedy people were very encouraged by the results of those TV campaign ads he ran in Massachusetts, appraising the response they drew in New Hampshire, which is where he lost before. They say this shows he is overcoming the so-called "personal issues." And so he is generally considered, and I suppose would be, the leading candidate.

Mondale seems to think that his people did very well this time with all the speaking he did around the country, and so does Gary Hart, all of them have been out on the campaign trail. I heard Alan Cranston, whom I hadn't been able to take very seriously although I like him. I thought there was an absence of charisma, which is what most observers think would do him in. I asked Harris Wofford, an old Kennedy hand, who has been working in his campaign, "Why do you think Alan has a chance?" He said, "Well, let me ask you something. If you think that Kennedy is not going to make it and Mondale is not going to make it, who's next? Who's got a better call on the nomination than Cranston, who's been a loyal leader in the Senate, has spoken all over the country for his colleagues and raised a lot of money?" And he reminded me of something I'd forgotten, that Cranston was reelected to the Senate in the 1980 Republican landslide and led Reagan in California by almost a million votes.

Finally I heard Cranston speak during the campaign in support of a candidate for the California state senate, and I saw a lot of charisma I hadn't seen before. He seems to have been reprogrammed. He has an absolutely great line that brought the house down: "People keep asking, 'Why do you think you should run for President?' and I always answer it in this way: California has given the nation three Presidents--Herbert Hoover, Richard Nixon, and Ronald Reagan--and I think I can do better than that."

QUESTION: I think he's forgotten one that I was thinking about. On a clear day from California, how do you see Lyndon Johnson's son-in-law, Chuck Robb, as a possibility in any way in 1984?

MR. ASHMORE: We don't have clear days anymore. I don't know the governor; I knew Linda Byrd when she was a child, but I don't think that counts. I must say I've never posed as an expert on Virginia politics. I've always been baffled by it. I suppose the situation has been affected profoundly by the expansion of Washington into the upper end of the state. I still think of Virginia back in the Harry Byrd/Carter Glass days; and that Virginia is not here anymore, I'm reasonably certain.

NARRATOR: We feel very privileged that Harry Ashmore has been with us and we thank him very much.

THE PRESIDENT AND DEFENSE:
SCIENCE AND PRIORITIES

Admiral K. S. Masterson

NARRATOR: We are very pleased you have joined us for a discussion that follows an earlier visit to the Miller Center by Admiral Masternon nearly a year ago. We benefited so much that we were interested that it be repeated.

Nothing could be more timely than a discussion of trends and developments in modern weaponry. In this matter, everybody is his own Monday morning quarterback. Anyone who had held an M-1 for twenty-five minutes is, of course, an authority on the latest development in weaponry; but we felt that we ought at least to balance that known talent, which all of us have, with a little bit more professional talent from the Joint Chiefs of Staff. In his previous visit Admiral Masterson was introduced by his good and close friend, Hugh Kelly, who is Commonwealth Professor of Physics at the University. Before Professor Kelly repeats his introduction, I want to say that the second question—not the first which we hope you will ask after the rather brief introduction Admiral Masterson will give—is what have we learned from naval combat in Argentina in the South Atlantic.

MR. KELLY: It is a very great pleasure for me to welcome Admiral Kleber S. Masterson, Jr. Admiral Masterson has had a very interesting and illustrious career. He did his undergraduate work, as many eminent naval officers do, at the U.S. Naval Academy in Annapolis. In addition to his academic accomplishments at the Naval Academy he edited and published the Navy song book when he was there and I think this is a very important accomplishment. Following that he went to sea and several years later he was sent to the Navy's post-graduate school in Monterey, California, which is very well known as a technical school. Following a brief tour there, he was sent for three years to the new campus at the University of California at San Diego, where the University of California established a very eminent school of science at least equal to the science facilities at Berkeley. Admiral Masterson received his Ph.D. there in two years. He was the first Ph.D. graduate of that institution and his research in theoretical nuclear physics was very outstanding, perhaps the most outstanding work in nuclear physics done during the 1960s. Today it is still widely recognized and well referenced.

To the temporary loss of physics, he then proceeded to go to sea again and served as a line officer in the Navy for a period of time and since then has moved on into naval weapons systems. He has been an aide to the Secretary of the Navy, Graham Claytor, who has spoken here. Admiral Masterson's present job as Chief of SAGA, the Studies Analysis and Gaming Agency for the Joint Chiefs of Staff. It is a very great pleasure for us to present to you Admiral Kleber Masterson.

ADMIRAL MASTERSON: There are a few things I would like to mention as a lead into our conversation. The first thing I would like to do, though, is to thank you all for your hospitality tonight. This is a most enjoyable event for me.

Needless to say, my focus will be on national priorities, that is, why we need a strong defense, and in particular why this administration is pushing defense as hard as it is in spite of budget deficits, the downturn in our economy, cries that it is coming at the expense of social programs. Unfortunately, what we spend on defense is not a function of how much we would like to spend, but is really a function of how much our opponent is spending and what he is doing. If we had no opponent and if there were no one girding to do things in the world which we considered contrary to our national interests and dangerous to us as a nation, obviously we wouldn't have to spend nearly the sums we do. For example, over the last decade, the Soviets have been spending an increased amount every year, on the order of three or four percent every year; and we, in the last decade, actually spent less. In real buying power, we spent less in the first part of the decade and just barely built back in the last half of the decade to a level of ten years ago. So today the Soviets, for the last several years have been outspending us about fifty percent. Thanks to the innovativeness and the science and technology of this great country of ours, to a certain extent we have been able to outthink them. We have been able to do better with our dollars than we believe the Soviets do with their equivalent. But we can't fool ourselves that we can outthink them forever.

That's basically where our crisis is today, and many of us feel we really have a crisis. The Soviets right now graduate many more engineers than we do in this country, and while we do a better job of putting it all together, there is no question that we face an opponent who really intends to "take us on." Fortunately they are very conservative. I think deterring the Soviets doesn't necessarily mean that we have to have a force that equals them gun for gun or tank for tank or ship for ship. But it certainly means we must have a force that they believe is one with which they cannot tangle and end up with a post-conflict situation which favors them more than the pre-conflict period. In other words, we have to be sure that when they do the calculating, hopefully conservatively, of what might happen if they tangle with us, that they conclude that it's worse than if they didn't tangle with us. I might add when we do that calculation today, that's what we picture. But hopefully we both have a calculus that's conservative.

One of the things that I want to talk about is today's weaponry, what we are buying and why we are buying it. War games for the Joint Chiefs of Staff are one of my functions, and one of the functions of my team is to take all of the weaponry we have and are projected to have over the next several years and war game the war that we think is a possible conflict for which the national strategy directs that we should be prepared as a nation. We do everything from a conventional war, say in Europe, or starting in Iran and moving to Europe, or starting in Korea and moving to Europe, up through the strategic nuclear exchange.

The purpose of such war gaming is to gain insights into those aspects of our defense programs that aren't obvious when you compare numbers--such as numbers of weapons on each side--and so forth. We can integrate a lot more in our war games than we can integrate in our heads as we look at the number of weapons systems each side has.

We are probably the strongest advocates of a statement that war games are not predictions of war outcomes. History has examples both ways, and in hindsight you can usually find examples of war games that showed how the war would have come out had some senior officer not interjected and said, "No, that's not right, change it." This reportedly happened with the Japanese and the Battle of Midway. In a war game it is said that carriers were destroyed, and in the war game the Japanese admiral in charge restored the two carriers saying that was clearly an incorrect outcome. History proved the war games prophetic--not the admiral. We wargamers like that story, of course, but there are other examples of cases in which one could not predict how things would come out because leadership, tactics, the morale of your soldiers, weigh a lot more than any war games can capture. If you'd use conventional wargaming I'm not sure the Israelis would have attempted their raid on Entebbe. On the other hand, I have seen an excellent post-Entebbe raid analysis which shows how, indeed, if you break the raid down in small pieces you can use wargaming to show how the raid could succeed. The above limitations notwithstanding, we find that wargaming gives us valuable insights not otherwise available, and provides a useful tool to supplement our military judgment.

Back to our weaponry, we are finding now that we are spending a lot of money on new weaponry; and we are doing it for two reasons: replacement of average systems and to introduce new technology.

It probably doesn't come as a surprise to you because these things have been said before, but the Bl-B will replace the B52 that has been in service in the order of twenty-five years. Some of the people flying in those airplanes are flying in airplanes their fathers flew in. You know, for a nation that keeps an automobile maybe five or ten years and thinks it is really old at ten years, you are talking about the front line bomber in this technology age which is more than two decades old. The same thing is true of our warships. We now plan for a warship to last thirty-five years. We are planning to get forty-five years out of our carriers. Now that's more than a full career of a typical naval officer or enlisted man. So, we may even have a case of first, second and third generation all serving in the same ship.

Now, what we do there is we don't leave the same weaponry on it through those four decades. We will clearly have to modernize the ship. One of the principal things we will do over the life-span of the ship will be to replace its sensors and perhaps some of its weapons, to keep up with the changing technology of the threat.

When the B52 was created, for example, the principal weapon it had to encounter was a shell fired by a gun, a shell that would travel ballistically to the airplane and whose odds of hitting it were very small. Today, its principal threat are twofold: there are surface-launched missiles that will find it and home on it, and air-launched missiles that can be shot from an airplane looking down at it and will home on it. Now, to counter those we've got a large number of countermeasure devices in the plane designed to confuse the incoming missiles, hopefully we will never really find out which one will be better, the electronics in the plane or the electronics in the missile. But, it's that sort of thing which we have to constantly keep trying to stay ahead of.

I want to close my remarks with just a couple of statistics and I'll use my notes if I might so I don't mix them up. I'm going back to the subject of how much are we spending on defense and can we afford the sort of defense towards which we are building. In 1964, the defense budget was forty-two percent of the federal budget. This year's defense budget is twenty-five percent of the federal budget. The 1964 budget was eight percent of our gross national product, down from on the order of nine percent, compared to something like fifteen percent for the Soviet Union. This year it is six percent of our gross national product. In the past we have historically carried defense spending at nine percent of the gross national product and done it with ease. In the Vietnam war it bounced a little above that while we were funding the war. Unfortunately, much of it went to what we would call "expandables," things that we lost in battle.

The Soviets, in the meantime are outspending us by fifty percent. They are spending about fifteen percent of their GNP on their war machine. And, as we all know, right now the Soviets have put themselves in an economic box. They are not self-sufficient in grain, they have a real problem with their balance of payments, and they have a real tough hard currency problem now. In that sense, their defense expenditures are almost like war-time expenditures for them. The thing that's frightening is they have been doing it for ten years now.

I think at that I will stop with my prepared remarks and open the floor to questions. In particular, I will be glad to take on any question, if it is asked, about Argentina.

QUESTION: Could you comment on some of the weapons technology that was used in the South Atlantic?

ADMIRAL MASTERSON: With the modern weaponry we have got today, we have a situation where chance seems to play a very highly leveraged role. The Sheffield, for example, was reportedly destroyed by a single missile with a three hundred pound warhead. The Sheffield did not have modern anti-missile weaponry. She did have a missile system but I think the missile system was about a fifteen or twenty year old technology, and in that weather I doubt that she even saw that Exocet. I don't think the radars on that ship are automated and I would be very surprised if the crew even saw it with more than a few seconds to react.

Now, we have created a fair amount of weaponry in the modern years that can actually handle anti-ship missiles. But we in the U.S. Navy are just beginning to install some of the point defense weaponry that can handle it and to improve our area defense weaponry to the necessary level. In air warfare we have two categories of weaponry that are installed in ships. Area defense missiles are those missiles which can shoot down an attacking missile or bomber at a range that would prevent it from attacking, not only the ship from which the missile is fired but also other ships. Area defense missiles have a range of twenty to one hundred miles. Point defense or self defense weaponry are a family of weapons designed to protect the ship itself.

Those of you familiar with World War II will remember that we started World War II with almost nothing that was capable of shooting down an airplane, never mind a missile. Very shortly after the war started we brought in twenty millimeter and forty millimeter guns. We imported them from overseas because we hadn't developed them. We created a computer that would enable our five-inch guns to calculate where to aim shells against airplanes. The five-inch gun was, in effect, an area defense weapon. It fired a shell that was five inches in diameter and about ninety pounds. The twenty millimeter and forty millimeter were just small machine guns for self defense.

Today we have one-and two-stage missile systems capable of ranges out to one hundred miles to shoot down the bomber and the missile on their way in. Then for those that survive that we are now

55

deploying to the fleet four different technologies to defeat the missile in close, and we are developing a fifth technology. But we try to develop these things as inexpensively as we can. We have chaff and electronic decoys and infrared decoys. And we have deceptive countermeasures that actually will take the signal from the incoming missile, put a little twist on it, and transmit it back to the missile. The missile receives its reflected signal, doesn't realize the electronics has been playing games with it, and instead of aiming at the ship, aims at an imaginary target elsewhere in space.

With two other technologies, we have taken the Sparrow missile, which we have used in air-to-air combat for about fifteen years now, and we have a shipborne version with an automatic radar that detects an incoming target, checks its identification, and, if not a friend, fires a missile at it. And then finally we have a twenty millimeter gun that has its own radar, called the Phalanx. It will look at the incoming missile, and if the missile could hit the ship and it is traveling fast enough not to be a helicopter, the gun will engage the missile and shoot at it until the missile blows up. The gun fires a small projectile. It is about the size of the end of my finger, and the projectile will burrow into the incoming missile, hit the warhead and set the warhead off, so that it actually turns the warhead of the incoming missile against the missile and blows it up. We tested that very thoroughly. It sounds like something out of Buck Rogers, but I can assure you we've proven to ourselves it will work.

QUESTION: Can one assume or is it likely that the Argentines had intelligence on the Shefield's location?

ADMIRAL MASTERSON: I think the reason they found the Sheffield, and I am really guessing at this, is because the Sheffield was on radar picket duty. The Sheffield's role was something akin to what we did in World War II against the kamikaze. We put destroyers on station ahead of our forces to try to see the kamikazes in time for our own airplanes to be vectored to intercept. The destroyers that did that duty were very vulnerable. And I suspect the Sheffield was on such duty. As a result, she didn't have any airplanes overhead. The Harrier is a very good airplane, but the British do not have enough of them to keep them airborne all the time, and I would guess that didn't have one over the Sheffield. The Argentine that came out may have had information on where the Sheffield was. As a matter of fact, I think they sent a surveillance airplane out and saw it. What happens there is if you are on a surface ship you have a choice of being quiet and then you are hard to find, but then you can't see anything; or having your radar on and then you can see, but you are also easy to locate. If the airplane coming out has an intercept receiver and just listens for your radar, they can hear your radar before you can see them. Then what they do is they drop down below the horizon and they come on in some more, and they pop up,

56

look real quickly, drop down, come in some more, pop up, drop down. The missile was fired from about twenty miles out, which would have been the radar horizon. So, essentially, what that airplane might have done was to sneak right on in under the radar envelope of the Sheffield, set the missile off, and then pop right back down and go home. So it wasn't luck, if that's the way it happened. It was a well executed maneuver.

Unfortunately, with the small carriers the British have, they don't have the capability to provide airborne radar. When you put a radar up in the sky, the radar horizon doesn't bother you as much, and such a radar would have been able to see that airplane coming in. For example, with our carrier battle groups, we would have had our airborne radars out, we would have seen that airplane two hundred miles away and he would have had F-14s all over him long before he got in there. But in the case of the British they don't have those resources down there. They only have the small carriers. I happen to believe in the small carrier like the ones the British have, but on the other hand the other lesson you learn in warfare is if you are going to get in a fight it's better to have really overwhelming superiority in your local region. Your losses will be significantly less than his.

We went through a phase--I was systems analyst, so I can say this about ourselves--when Mr. McNamara came in, where he properly tried to make us become more quantitative about what we were doing. But unfortunately, we began to believe some of our calculations too much. In particular, we began to believe the calculation which tried to figure out how we get just enough defense that if we go to war we will end up with one soldier left with one bullet in his rifle. I'm being unfair--it wasn't quite that bad. The lesson we have learned from history is that if you are going to get in a fight, if you have the option of having an overwhelming superiority, you are going to take a lot fewer losses. It's going to be a lot quicker and your losses will be fewer. As a matter of fact, if you have such overwhelming superiority there is even a chance you won't have to get in a fight. As an aside, those who study history tell me, that if you go over the offensive actions over the last couple of hundred years or more, you will find almost always the side which attacks wins. But, if you analyze it, the attacker had such a force or tactical advantage that he had reason to believe he'd win, and to this he frequently added the advantages of surprise. The lesson the historian wanted to teach is that the side which goes on the offensive wins. The lesson I learned was that a nation usually won't go on the offensive until it thinks it will win, which says to me that for us, in a free world where we don't plan to be the ones who are the aggressors, that we owe it to ourselves to have enough capability that no other nation will think it will win. That's not necessarily enough to "win" an offensive war.

QUESTION: I have maintained that the Soviet Union and the United States have sufficient nuclear weapons to totally annihilate each other, regardless of whom makes the first strike, and the question that comes up time and time again is why are we pouring more and more money into expensive weapons if we already have sufficient stockpiles to destroy each other, regardless of whom initiates the attack.

ADMIRAL MASTERSON: We both have enough weapons that if we targeted them on each other's cities we would destroy each other's population. In the days of mutual assured destruction, or MAD, that was indeed our strategic philosophy. That is to say, we would target Soviet cities, we would target their economic and military recovery potential. But basically, the philosophy in those days of very inaccurate weapons was that we held each other's populations hostage and that would lead to mutual deterence because neither of us wanted it to happen. I don't believe either we or the Soviets today are trying to destroy each other's population. And to destroy each other's war fighting potential-frankly we don't have enough weapons to do that. We have enough weapons to do very severe, but, we believe, not enough damage to each other's war fighting, capability. For example, let's consider the silos from which their missiles are launched. The Soviets have a capability of reloading some of their silos. If we want to target their silos, it takes a lot of weapons. We think the Soviets are targeting all our silos. Further, the Soviets are going underground and hardening many elements of their warfighting capability. As a matter of fact, they are hardening their silos, too. The Soviets are hardening almost everything of value to them, and it takes more capable weapons to attack such targets. They also have very impressive evacuation plans and shelters for their population.

Parenthetically, we don't have such well developed plans and don't have such shelters, which worries some of us who look at the strategic balance. It concerns us that they may do the calculus and say "Ah ha, we could destroy that nation." If that were to happen, if I were a Soviet analyst looking at that war, I worry that I might start thinking that war was winnable, that I might do so much damage to the U.S. versus the damage they would do to us, the Soviets, that I might not be as deterred from that escalation as we would like them to be. One of my jobs is the calculation of how many weapons is enough. I can tell you when I do the calculation in accordance with strategic guidance, we are far short of that number, and what we are building makes very good sense.

Interestingly enough, all of the Chiefs, in the face of that statement, still believe it is in our national interest to have a mutual reduction of nuclear weapons. What they think is important is that it be a mutual reduction, even though the asymmetries between us suggest that the Soviet may benefit relative to us if we reduce weapons, because it takes fewer weapons to do a given amount of damage to the United States than it does to the same amount of damage to the Soviet Union. The Chiefs have been strong supporters of strategic arms reduction. But what worries them is that it has to be mutual and it has to be verifiable. That's the crunch.

QUESTION: The Hughes employee's espionage involves so many of our defense secrets. Have you any indication of the damage that was done to our weapons systems developments?

ADMIRAL MASTERSON: I don't know personally and if I knew I probably couldn't say. The few things I think I know a little about that he divulged could hurt us very, very seriously because they could affect some things that right now are highly classified.

QUESTION: What about the Stealth bomber and the amount of information that could have been divulged to the Soviets relative to a decision: do you go to B-1s, or do you wait out the Stealth, or just where do you go? I drove B-52's for quite a number of years so I am a little curious about the transition.

ADMIRAL MASTERSON: Let me answer that in several parts. What happened was a Hughes employee has given away, apparently sold, to the Russians one heck of a lot of defense information he was privy to, including reportedly some information about our Stealth technology. This is the technology that enables you to build missiles and bombers that are very much harder for radars to see because they either absorb the radar energy or reflect it in such a way that they look to a radar a fraction of the size that they really are. And I'm talking about a bomber that can be made to look as small as, maybe, a bird. I might add the Soviets were the first ones to examine theoretically the technology and the physics. We apparently were the first ones to put it in practice, or to try to put it in practice. But, if it's speeded up the Soviet acquisition of that technology, it would be of grave concern to me as a designer of defensive weaponry because a missile that was nearly invisible would be a very formidable foe, which would take changes in our weaponry to accommodate. There isn't anything out there now that the modern weaponry can't handle, and that includes some things with very small cross sections.

On the other side of that, in terms of the B-1 and the Stealth bomber, let me just say a couple of words on that. There is a syndrome where if we try to introduce something to the fleet today, and we try to develop something for introduction maybe in four or five years, and then something that might be five years after that, what we find happens is that the people who don't want us to introduce the thing today say, "If you've got this better thing coming in five years let's not do the thing today." And that "usually" saves a lot of money because one can show how he is really improving defense by causing us to focus more on a better technology that will come later. Indeed, if you can guarantee no war would happen in the next five years maybe that's a better way to do it. Then of course the one who doesn't like the technology five years from now argues you've got to see the better one coming five years after that.

We had this happen in the Navy with something called the LAMPS helicopter. We discovered that helicopters are very good submarine fighters because they can reposition rapidly. The way anti-submarine warfare goes, all of a sudden you might get a short contact with a submarine, and then lose it again. Something that can move rapidly to the scene and put some sonobuoys down and find it again and then attack it is very valuable. Admiral Zumwalt, when he was Chief of Naval Operations, liked the concept so much that he took a number of utility helicopters that were already in the fleet and he modified them to carry a torpedo and off-the-shelf detection and communications equipment. Then he modified destroyers that had helicopter decks; by giving them enough equipment they could operate the LAMPS helicopter. This was a really low cost way to take what was basically a utility helicopter and make it into part of our weapons system. And that was called LAMPS I-light airborne multi-purpose system. And then somebody said, "Well, that was not a bad idea, Admiral, but what you really should have done is let us design avionics specifically for that role because this off-the-shelf electronics doesn't do nearly as well as you could do." So we would have something called LAMPS II, which will be available in about five years: an upgraded LAMPS I. That seemed like a great idea so we started to do that also. Then somebody said, "But you know, really, that helicopter is quite old and it's not really designed for that task, it doesn't go very far and it doesn't stay up very long. The army is developing a new helicopter to transport their troops, an assault helicopter, and we could go with the army and buy some of those helicopters. They'd have much longer endurance and then you could really have a proper LAMPS." Thus, quite logically, we had a sequential program: LAMPS I, LAMPS II, and LAMPS III. As an analyst in the Navy's Office of Systems Analysis, I can assure you we had a very good cost effectiveness argument for that program, but we didn't have a good political argument. We discovered what was happening was just what I described. LAMPS II was killing LAMPS I; LAMPS III was killing LAMPS II; the proponents of LAMPS I were killing LAMPS III--it was wild. We were about to lose them all. Finally Admiral Zumwalt figuratively took a pistol and put it to the head of LAMPS II and shot it. He said, "There is no more LAMPS II; we have LAMPS I which is 'now' and LAMPS III which is ten years from now, and nobody can argue that we should kill the program for today with one that is ten years away."

Unfortunately, the Air Force with a Stealth bomber and the B1-B are getting into this LAMPS II-LAMPS III argument. As a ship

60

driver I have no reason to be arguing for airplanes, but I can assure you that as an analyst, from the strategic war games, I see a lot of leverage from Bl-B, and I think the program makes sense. That's a personal opinion.

I also see, of course, a good case for the Stealth bomber, because I think with that technology, it makes sense for this country to be the first country to deploy it. The only thing that I would remark is that our history of deploying new technologies is a checkered one, and I'd argue that the Stealth bomber is the bush, the Bl-B being the bird in the hand, because we know now how to build them. When I game the strategic war, there are two things about the bomber that I like. One of them is just that it is another technology for which the other side has to account.

We have had for years, as you all know, a Triad concept. We wanted to be sure that we had three different technologies so that we wouldn't be surprised and discover one day that a countermeasure had made our strategic deterrent obsolete. And I frankly believe that is a smart way to go. We just don't know that much about the future. We don't know absolutely what the Russians are doing; we just don't dare put all our eggs in any one basket, including the submarine basket, which today seems to be the most survivable and the most stable; its the one that gives you the feeling that we do not have to react instantly. But on the other hand, even though we have been studying anti-submarine warfare very well, and we think we are way ahead of the Russians, and we don't think there is anything they can do to get those submarines, we just don't dare put all our eggs in that basket because of that uncertain future.

The other thing about the Bl is that it may well be the one leg of the triad that deters them the most. You launch it and you've got lots of time to decide whether or not it's to go in and attack. That's one good thing about it. And if it does go in, they really don't know what it is going to find or where it is going to attack. Whereas the missiles are going to attack fixed targets whose position we know. I think it adds a dimension to the deterrence that missiles, alone, don't have. And again, in spite of the cost of the very expensive bombers, and even though I am a missilier, I believe in having a man up there in that process.

QUESTION: What would you say to Congressman Aspin who rejected the freeze and then said, "The interesting thing about SALT II is that we have been following everything in it. If we look at the Reagan defense budget, big as it is, there is not one single weapon that we are proposing to get started or anything that is inconsistent with SALT II; everything that Ronald Reagan wants to do, that the Pentagon wants to do, we could do under SALT II."

ADMIRAL MASTERSON: That's a good point Congressman Aspin makes about SALT II. The interesting thing about a treaty is that one shouldn't negotiate a treaty unless one believes that there is mutual benefit in the outcome, because history shows treaties are observed when both parties believe the treaty is mutually beneficial. SALT I has expired and we are adhering to SALT I.   SALT II was not ratified, but indeed we are deactivating nuclear submarines as the Tridents go to sea, and the Soviets have cut up their submarines as they have introduced their newer ballistic submarines.   So, indeed, adherence to SALT II is actually involving a decommissioning of strategic weapons systems by both sides.

Aspin's point then would be: why don't we ratify SALT II?   I believe what the Reagan administration is saying is SALT II didn't go far enough, and certainly the President's proposal goes well beyond Salt II.   What he is saying is, "I don't want to take the time to arm wrestle with that, I want to get on to pushing farther into it." From where I stand, as long as both sides are adhering to what appears to be in our mutual interests, I would agree with the Reagan administration.   The key to why is it in our mutual interest to negotiate reduction in arms, of course, is that history shows arms races don't benefit either side.   And, I think on the U.S. side there is a very strong perception on the part of all of us in uniform that this country can afford the defense we need to match the Russians.   I submit this country can afford to stay ahead of the Russians on the military side, and I think it's inconceivable that we wouldn't.

Nonetheless, we feel that it is hard on this country.   Most of us are very conservative about the budget and are very uncomfortable about the budget deficit.   We are hurt by inflation because inflation means that, among other things, our weaponry prices usually go up faster than anybody else's costs.   We feel very strongly that what it does is that it eats into our ability to buy the things we need.   From the point at which we and the Congress agree on what it is that the Congress will provide to the time when we pay the bills and the products are delivered, we frequently find that inflation has eaten away some of our buying power.   Not all of it is restored by the Congress, so that inflation, in effect, costs us weapons.   And it also, I might add, gives Senator Proxmire his quarterly chance to take a barb at us because, of course, we report our cost growth in all our weapons systems.   And even though we identify what we believe is due to inflation, it still makes much better press to make a big thing out of how much it is.   By the way, our control over cost growth is pretty remarkable.   I believe something like one or two percent of our contracts actually experience cost growth.   Admittedly every now and then when we experience it, it's a big one and it is dramatic sometimes embarrassing.   And, of course, sometimes its growth does reflect poor management on our part.

Another thing that you see when you see the newspaper headlines about how we've made our quarterly report to Congress in our weapons systems and we've had all of this growth in it, quite frequently what you will see included in that growth is another year of projection. That then gets carried as a cost growth for that system, even though what it really is is just now looking another year ahead and knowing that we are going to buy another fifty tanks or whatever. So you need to read between the lines pretty carefully when you receive the reports on "Pentagon Reports Record Cost Growth," etc.

QUESTION: What is your feeling about building large carriers? At an earlier session, Robert Komer former deputy secretary of defense, brought up this question. Because of the long time required for the building of carriers, the cost overruns, the delays, and by the time--I forget the number of years, quite a few years--the carrier was launched, it was outmoded, obsolete. I was just wondering what your opinion is: should one pursue that enormous expenditure on big ships like aircraft carriers, or should we concentrate more on those anti-missile missiles you were talking about, and defense mechanisms to protect us from a first strike? Senator Hart versus the secretary of the navy.

ADMIRAL MASTERSON: I think both are right. That's the funny thing about it. I participated in the Navy's and Admiral Zumwalt's, effort to sell the Hill on building the smaller carrier. It was the Hill that killed it. Of all places, it was the House Appropriations Committee. Admiral Zumwalt believed that we ought to be producing a family of small carriers that carry Harriers and helicopters and would protect convoys--they'd be like the CVS of World War II--among other things. As I'll discuss in a minute, there is a real case for them.

On the other hand, even for a case such as the Falklands, it is a little bit too big of a fight for this carrier to be big enough. If the U.S. were down there, I think we would want to have a large carrier even if we had the small ones; I think we would feel they weren't enough and we'd send a big carrier down if that were our fight.

We did the analysis for the small carrier when I was in the Office of Systems Analysis, and made a prediction of how well the small carrier would work. We then took one of our amphibious ships that could carry Harriers and helicopters, and we sent them out under our Operational Test and Evaluation Force, which is completely independent entity, and we tested the concept. We actually went out and set up exactly the same situation with our submarines acting as Soviet submarines, that we had used in our computer simulations. In our cost effectiveness analysis that we sent to the Hill we predicted a level of effectiveness and showed that these carriers should be built. In the hands of the fleet they outperformed our analysis, so they were even better in reality than we were claiming in our analyses. And it was because of certain synergisms-well, I'll tell you an anecdote. The Harrier was just supposed to be an anti-air and ground attack airplane. The anti-submarine work was to be done by the helicopter that would fly out on each side ahead of the convoy and would drop sonobuoys in the water. As the convoy moved ahead, the helicopter also moved ahead and put a buoy further out and so on, the idea being that the nuclear submarine that was trying to intercept the convoy would have to drive through those buoys. The helicopter would hear the submarine and then attack it, and you could launch another helicopter to go help with the attack. Well, what we found happened in the actual case was that we would be going along and the helicopter would drop a sonobuoy, and occasionally he would hear something. He would have to go back and circle around and drop more buoys to find out what it was--it might just be a false target. But meanwhile he wasn't laying his next sonobuoy, so there was a hole in his screen. The other helicopter wasn't fast enough to get out there and fill the hole. So the sailors used the Harrier, which was very fast. The Harrier is the British airplane that takes off straight up and then flies wherever you want to fly and then can land straight down. It is a very useful airplane. The Harrier pilot had some sonobuoys in the cockpit; he took off, flew out to the position for the next sonobuoy; and threw one over the side. That keep screen integrity while the helicopter was doing his thing. We didn't claim that in our analysis, it was the good old U.S. sailor with his inventiveness who dreamed up that idea.

QUESTION: How do you feel about the reliability of these very high-technology systems? We have so much problem with equipment being down, spare parts and all that sort of thing. We've got these capabilities, but are they really going to be dependable?

ADMIRAL MASTERSON: That's a very good question. But, I didn't finish answering the last question so let me pick up two questions. I believe in the big carrier because first, you have to get to a certain size before you can really absorb hits by these gigantic weapons the Soviets are firing. Unfortunately in war I think there has to be some element in your force that can just stand up and slug it out. The small light forces are great for jabbing and counter-punching, etc., but unfortunately, in war, I think eventually you just have to be able to slug it out with the other guy. You know, the only airplane that anybody owns, Air Force or Navy, that can intercept Soviet bombers before they can launch those missiles at us, is the F14 which has the Phoenix missile that can be fired a good fifty miles. All the other weaponry and all the other free world airplanes, fire only five or ten miles. And those big airplanes need a big carrier. Frankly, I think the U.S. Navy needs both. I think we need the big ones that can go in and slug it out if that's necessary, and they need the small ones that can fill in the cracks and do the things elsewhere.

Back to the question of reliability. About eight years ago the U.S. Navy hired from NASA a man by the name of Mr. Willoughby, whose sole job was to make us pay attention to the sort of reliability that we used in our space program. We've learned an awful lot since then about how you design it in and build it into your systems. For example, I was describing the Phalanx system. You all know the stories of development systems where the complaint is that the engineers are in there playing around with it before they test it, and what does it prove, because what sailor will not know how to do that sort of adjusting. I happened to be out to watch one very important test of Phalanx, and I went down to watch what the engineers would do in preparing this very sophisticated system for the test. There is a built-in test there that is run by the computer in the gun, and one literally punches a few buttons and it tells you if the system is O.K. That's all the engineer did on the day of the test. I know because we left the system on the ship overnight with nobody aboard ship; we flew out to the ship that morning, ran the test and flew back. So, we have reached the point now where, in many of our systems, we can build these tests that can tell the sailor whether the system works or not, and if it isn't working can tell them which card or say one out of two or three cards he should replace. That's what modern computer technology has done for us. Fifteen years ago if you had a built-in test system like that, odds are that the failure would have been in the test set and you wouldn't have trusted it.

Now a second part of your question, though, is availability. I'm saying now that if we can find the problem and if we have the part we can fix it in less than an hour in most cases. Furthermore these systems typically run tens of days before they fail. But on the other hand, the spare parts is the question because we can't afford to carry every part. We have a rule that seems very simple for our ships. It says that if a part is expected to fail on a ship once in four years, we will have it aboard. That sounds like an incredibly generous rule except, oddly enough, it works out that the state of the art radars, which are high power electronic devices, run about two hundred to four hundred hours between failures. If you do the mathematics it works out that you can't afford enough spare parts because of the thousands of different parts that can contribute to that failure every two hundred hours. You can't afford enough spare parts on every ship to have every part that is going to fail. And so it works out that maybe eighty percent of the time we have the part that is going to fail but that twenty percent of the time the part isn't there, and the sailor has a long wait for the part. And when you take that into account, plus some underfunding in past years, you see availability in the fleet down on our new systems on the order of seventy percent sometimes and on old systems down as low as fifty percent. So, I'm saying two things: first, the answer is partially "no." Some of the equipment is not going to be available. On the other hand we are getting very much better than we used to because we are using technology in a conscious program to improve the availability. Nonetheless, it's a war we haven't yet won.

QUESTION: Was it availability or reliability that stopped the helicopter raid in Iran?

ADMIRAL MASTERSON: I believe that was an inflight reliability problem, that is a failure of equipment in flight. I believe the way that story goes was that there were eight helicopters in the squadron on the ship. And, the calculus they had to make was "was the risk worth taking with the eight on hand?" It was not possible to get more helicopters of that particular type in a timely fashion. That calculus looked pretty good. But, there was a finite risk one would have to take. I think when they launched they had six maybe, so they had two that weren't available for launch. My guess is what they did is that they ended up stealing parts from those to make sure the six they launched were all right. Then they lost two in flight. They had to have five for the last part of the rescue effort, I believe. Anyway, what happened was one of the ones they lost enroute in that bad sandstorm, that had to turn around and go back, had some of the spare parts that would have been needed to fix one that went down at the intermediate landing point, so they decided they couldn't go on from there. I haven't read Admiral Holloway's investigation of the rescue effort, so many facts may not be correct.

QUESTION: Do you think the consolidation of the various branches of the military services hopefully might have some economic savings? If we are going to be using missiles, it looks like we could maybe come down to one or two branches of service instead of three or four?

ADMIRAL MASTERSON: I am now in the Joint Staff and I am very impressed with the functioning of that body. I didn't think I would be when I went there, but I really am. The staff that serves the Joint Chiefs, the Office of the Joint Chiefs of Staff, is multi-service manned. And of course the Chairman in recent days has been making headlines by suggesting that in the future it would serve this country well if the Chairman of the Joint Chiefs had more power and if the staff served him more directly. I make two statements: That staff he's got will serve him any way he wants them to serve him. But, my second statement is, that I am not sure. I disagree with some of what he wants in terms of, in wartime or even in peacetime, the command of our armed forces, the forces in the field, going through identifiable, responsible, accountable people. I believe you ought to keep responsibility, accountability, and authority together. Even though I think the Chiefs do a fantastic job, there is some value in the command of our forces to have a strong line through the Chairman, which I believe in fact has happened historically anyway.

In terms of planning and programming for the armed forces, the budgeting, in terms of peacetime employment of forces, I think the country is well served by the system we have now. I think the Canadian experience in unifying all services under one uniform hasn't worked that well.

I don't believe there would be savings that would be accrued from it. In my last job I had a number of joint programs with the Army. I found I was proposing more joint programs as a Naval officer than the system was ready to absorb, because I saw it in the Navy's interest. I saw the Army having better technology some places than we, in gun ammunition and gunnery, for example. They were spending more than we were going to be able to afford and my feeling was, fine, let's go with the Army. I already had one joint project with them on something called the guided projectile. At the time I was in charge of the development of the Navy gun programs. My feelings were very simple: I couldn't afford it; they could. Let's see if they won't meet our needs, which they were quite willing to do.

I think the economics is the problem. Since Secretary Laird was secretary of defense, and in effect convinced the Services that they were going to be given a lot of say in how they divided their budgets, we have been very conscious within our own Services of the fact that there are limited dollars and what we spend on A we wouldn't have available for B. We have gone through very heavy trade-offs internally in order to get the most for our dollar. That's very real, that has been going on, as I say, since that time, incidentally using many of the tools that we learned from Mr. McNamara. The argument that we fight for missions that belong to each other, I don't believe that happens as much as people believe. Frankly, I think some competition has been very healthy. There was a phase there, for example, when the Air Force tactical people had almost all their war planes and missiles coming from the Navy because the Navy-developed systems were better. I think it was in the national interest that it came that way, but it took a competition between Air Force and Navy systems. Next time it may be that they will do a better job of development than we do.

Now there are some secretaries of defense who try to legislate commonality, for example--the famous F-lllB. And the problem was they tried to legislate it from on high rather than make sure that it really makes sense from below. The F-lllB was a case where the secretary of defense decreed that the Navy would use the Air Force-developed F-lll as its next fighter. The Navy really didn't want that airplane, parochially to begin with, but also because they really didn't believe it would work, and for a very interesting reason. One of the first things Admiral Zumwalt did as a young flag officer in the Navy was to head a study of the F-lllB. The interesting thing we found was: yes, if it would perform as the company was promising us it would perform, we did want it because of the weapon system on it, the Hughes Phoenix missile system. That's the system that makes it today the only airplane in the world that can handle the Soviet Backfire bomber before it can launch its anti-ship missiles. It's the longest range airborne weapon system in the world. Any airplane that can carry that weapon system was worth buying, if the airplane could fly off the carrier.

Well, it turned out later the F-111B grew heavier and in its first tests in carrier landings it broke its landing gear. That was not considered a safe way to land! The reason this weight growth happened was because it was not built the way a Navy airplane is, with a keel. A navy airplane is grabbed by a catapult and is thrown off the ship by its nose wheel. So, all of the weight of the airplane has to be carried through a keel to that nose wheel. Then when it lands, it's caught by an arresting gear which grabs a hook on the rear of the plane. So, carrier aircraft are built with a keel that runs the length of the plane to carry all these stresses. The F-111B had an internal bomb bay which was a nice big square cut out in the middle of the airplane, and all the stresses had to be carried around the corners of that bomb bay. Then, in addition, they had an enclosed compartment for the pilot and copilot who sat side by side in a capsule that could be ejected from the airplane if the airplane got in trouble. That, too, was a box, and all the stresses had to go around that. So it was a mechanical problem, and it failed on that mechanical problem.

Just to finish the tale, it turned out the F-111B was to be a General Dynamics airplane, but Grumman Aircraft Company was to be their subcontractor and would build the Navy version. Grummond had built navy airplanes for years. Grumman came to the Navy with an unsolicited proposal for an airplane that would carry the Phoenix system. Of course, it was the F-111 with a keel.

In sum, I believe we benefit from having separate Services. Healthy competition has helped make our nation the strongest in the world.

NARRATOR: Thank you for a most illuminating and informative discussion of scientific and defense issues.

THE PRESIDENT, THE PEOPLE AND A STRATEGY
FOR NATIONAL DEFENSE

Admiral Harry D. Train, II

NARRATOR: As all of you know, we are here at Monticello thanks to George Palmer and the Thomas Jefferson Memorial Foundation. We feel privileged every time there is an opportunity to entertain a distinguished guest at Monticello. We try not to take advantage but to aim very high with the people that we do invite. That's the case today with Admiral Harry D. Train, II. He has a distinguished naval career which he began as a graduate of the U.S. Naval Academy; he received his commission in 1949 and rose in rank to Admiral by 1978.

Mr. Jefferson put stress on theory and practice in his career, alternately going into the political field and then returning to think long thoughts and plan broad strategies and actions. In reviewing Admiral Train's biography the same trait manifests itself. He has had several very key and crucial command assignments, beginning with serving as Commander of the cruiser-destroyer Flotilla 8 in 1971 and 1972. He was Commander of the Sixth Fleet in 1976-1978. He became Commander of the U.S. Atlantic Fleet and Supreme Allied Commander of the Atlantic Fleet in 1978 and has held that position to the present time.

At the same time throughout his career he has also served in headquarters and in planning bodies, such as a few of the following: He was Director of the International Security Affairs Office in the East Asian and Pacific Office of the Assistant Secretary of Defense; he was Director of Systems Analysis of the Division Outsystems Analysis in the Office of the Chief of Naval Operations from 1973 to 1974; he was Director of the Joint Staff in the organization of Joint Chiefs of Staff from 1974 to 1976. He has received numerous decorations: the DSM with two gold stars, the Legion of Merit with three gold stars, the Meritorious Service Medal, the Joint Service Commendation Medal, and various international decorations including the Order of the Republic of Tunisia, the Order of Naval Merit from Brazil, and similar awards from the governments of Uruguay and Chile. It is an honor to have you with us, Admiral Train.

ADMIRAL TRAIN: Thank you. The subject that I have been asked to address tonight is a very difficult one to cover. Perhaps it is not so much that it is difficult to address as much as it is not a very well understood subject. It is not understood by the military the nation holds accountable for its security. And it is not understood by the political leadership. You can back into the subject, or you can get into the subject all at once. I think I will follow the latter course.

I have a role model who has been very important to me in recent years. He was General George S. Brown who was the Chairman of the Joint Chiefs of Staff at the time I was Director of the Joint Staff. General Brown was a very controversial chairman, but among those who knew him, he was a very loved man. He was a very wise man who always said what he thought, and he understood things very well. Sometimes when he talked about those things that he understood well, he offended people. Nonetheless he understood them and he was able to describe that feeling quite well. One of the things that troubled him continuously through the course of his more senior years was the relationship between the military and the political leadership of the nation. He became so obsessed with what he perceived to be a breakdown in understanding of what we are talking about tonight--the relationship between the presidency/political leadership and the military--that he went to great lengths to describe this to everybody who would listen to him. There is a quote I would like to share with you that describes it very succinctly. He gave this speech from which I am quoting the year he died: "The American military has no separate life of its own. It is not an end in itself but is simply a means to an end of protecting and preserving our national security. In the final analysis it is the American people who determine our national goals and objectives, including the defense and security of our nation. The armed forces are the instrument of the people, they are constituted and supported by the elected representatives of the people and serve to achieve national goals. And what that service shall consist of is decided by the people and their elected representatives. How they perform that service, on the other hand, has always been and must always be a matter of pride, patriotism, professionalism, and integrity for the individual military man and for the entire fraternity of arms he represents." That is an extremely important, succinct and accurate statement of the relationship between the military and the political leadership. It applies directly to the context of your subject for tonight, "The Military and the Presidency."

While the track record of this nation is not really brilliant in coming to grips with what the political leadership does as opposed to what the military leadership does, we are very fortunate in having available to us today (by us I mean both the political leaders and the military leaders) a very sound and stable set of national objectives, and we have a very sound body of law and customs and usage that tell us how the military will relate with the presidency and with our political leaders. As you all know, Article II, Section 2 of the Constitution specifically designates the President as the Commander in Chief of the Armed Forces. It specifically reads, "Commander in Chief of the Navy and Army." There is no doubt about it--he is Commander in Chief. And there is no doubt about what the term implies.

The same article gives authority to the Congress, to the Senate, specifically, on the subject of appointments and other constraints on the presidency's authority as Commander in Chief. Congress, on the other hand, has a role that is described in Article One, Section 8 which reads approximately as follows: The Congress shall have the power to raise and support armies.   The wording is "raise and support armies."   It specifically says that there will be no appropriation relative to the Army that will extend more than two years.   In the same section Congress is authorized and directed to provide and maintain a navy.

But the Constitution is not all that specific in the treatment of the armed forces.   Ideally for those of us that have to execute policy, and for those of us who have to fight when challenged, the President should establish our political objectives and make political decisions.   Or, more specifically, The presidency should establish political objectives and make political decisions.   The Congress should provide the assets with which we carry out those decisions and with which we pursue those political objectives, and the military should provide the advice and provide the skills, the professional military skills, and the execution of those policies.   Ideally that's the way it should work.

As practice would have it, as the years go by, as the identity of leaders change, as we have strong political leaders and weak military leaders, or strong military leaders and weak political leaders, these lines blur somewhat and the authorities and the practice of making decisions and executing those decisions migrates from one category of authority to another.   It never fails.   I've never known a time in recent history where there has not been both an exceeding of official authority and migrating of that authority from one department or one authority to another.   The dominant element in this spirited process of establishing policies, making political decisions, providing assets, and carrying out or executing tasks, is a political objective.   This is not well understood.   A political objective is a dominant element in the relationship between the presidency and the military.   And without political objectives our military objectives are worthless, absolutely worthless.   The military must be used solely for the purpose of achieving political objectives.

When I describe the presidency, what I really mean and what we have to understand, is that the presidency is not only the man, the President, it is the national command authority as described in the National Security Act of 1947.   The presidency, in that context, articulates the political objectives in a variety of ways, but the way that has the most impact on the system today is in a document called the Defense Guidance.   The Defense Guidance is drafted and promulgated by the secretary of defense. To us it is very important because it tells us really what to do.   It conveys the presidency's

71

political objectives, its goals, its decisions, to those the military people who have to carry them out. I am not talking about day-to-day decisions, I am talking about the decisions that affect the whole strategy of a nation.

I want to share with you what today's Defense Guidance tells us are the national security objectives of the United States, the political objectives, that affect both the military and the security of the nation. Those national security objectives are specifically and precisely as follows: (1) to deter attack on the United States, its allies and its friends; (2) to prevent the coercion of the United States, its allies, and its friends; (3) to protect U.S. economic interests and U.S. citizens abroad; (It's the first time U.S. citizens abroad have been mentioned since Defense Guidance has been published.) (4) to maintain access to petroleum supplies and other critical resources (by that is meant access to those resources we get from the southern parts of Africa and which are so vital to the industrial process in the United States); and(5) to reverse the geographic expansion of Soviet control and military presence throughout the world. That is the entire body of our national security objectives as given to us, the unified commanders of the armed forces of the United States. They are easy to understand.

But what we ought to question, when taken as a whole, is the importance of identifying and articulating, and then reacting to the vital interests of the United States. We as a nation are not very skilled in identifying our vital interests. We react historically in a rather spasmodic way to challenges. Very seldom can we specifically identify vital interests and how our military forces might be used to defend those vital interests.

When the vital interests are clear the task assigned to the military is very easy. Let me give you an example. When the Carter administration decided that U.S. access to oil in the Middle East was threatened, they were aware the only force with which we could react to that threat was the Navy, our maritime forces. The Presidency directed us to establish in the Indian Ocean a dominant maritime presence. The political objective was clearly stated. It was to establish such maritime dominance in the Indian Ocean as to deny to the political leadership of the Soviet Union any option requiring support from the sea. This is all our nation had the capability to do. That's what the Carter administration directed us to do.

We did not have adequate forces to accomplish this so we in the military leadership had to tell the Presidency that if it wanted to carry this out it would require a force equal to two carrier battle groups and we would have to divert that force from someplace else where it was currently employed defending other vital interests. The presidency said, "All right, do that." So we took one carrier battle group from the Mediterranean and we took one carrier battle group from the Western Pacific, and put them both into the Indian Ocean. The first carrier that I sent there, my contribution, was the U.S.S. Nimitz a nuclear-powered aircraft carrier. We sent that carrier and its nuclear powered escorts from the Mediterranean all the way around Africa to the Indian Ocean where it stayed without ever going into port. It finally returned to its home port in Norfolk eight months and four days after its departure.

Now that operating tempo borders on the challenges and the hardships that were imposed upon our whaling ship crews back in the 1800s. It was a very, very lengthy deployment. The U.S.S. Eisenhower relieved the Nimitz. The Eisenhower left Norfolk and returned about eight months and seven days later, having spent four days in port in that entire period. I met both ships out at sea when they came back, talked to the crews, talked to the officers, talked to the pilots of the Air Group. Everybody was happy. Why were they happy? Because they knew why they were there. They thought that they were making an important contribution to defending the vital interests of the United States. They understood exactly why they had gone out there. It was easy for them to understand. It was a big step. The retention rates stayed high, there were no behavior problems before, during or after the cruise. It was an ideal situation in that it was clearly articulated to the crew why they were doing this, why they were suffering the separation from their family and their homes. And they valued the fact that they were counted upon to do this job. Really, that sounds unusual but it is true. There wasn't a single problem.

Back in the Vietnam War, on the other hand, we had all the problems that go along with not being able to identify the vital interests of the nation or not being able to tell people why they are dying, why they are separated from their families, and why they are hiding around the jungle carrying out a policy that they did not understand. That is not to say that we didn't have vital interests in Vietnam, we were not very skilled and articulate in saying what those interests were. We really suffered from that. The book written by Maxwell Taylor that bears the title The Uncertain Trumpet clearly describes the phenomena of not knowing our vital interests and not knowing why we are sending people to do a difficult job. You all probably know it borrows from a biblical phrase that says, "if the trumpet blows an uncertain note who shall know where the battle lies?" It is as true today as it was back in biblical times.

Now, I will say one more thing about Vietnam and then leave it forever because it is a dangerous subject for us. The military were guilty in the case of Vietnam of taking carelessness on the part of the political leadership and employing it to the advantage of the military.

We probably came as close to exceeding the threshold of tolerance on the migration of the lines of authority back and forth between departments in the case of Vietnam as at any point in our recent history. This is articulated fairly well by a young Army colonel who wrote an article for the Naval Institute. It was never published but I was on the editorial board at the time the article was submitted and I robbed from it this quote. It is very appropriate. In order that I will not be guilty of plagarism I mention that the colonel's name was W. F. Long. These are his words, not mine: "Vietnam will have paid for itself only if we learned the lesson that techniques are not strategy, data are not facts, and management is not leadership." That in a nutshell, to me anyway, describes the entire military involvement in Vietnam, and all the abuses of which the military is guilty.

Because in that period of time we lacked that clear political direction, or a comprehension of what the direction was, we were really running a rudderless military operation. There is a very sound rule among the many rules that Clausewitz conveys to us in his writings that military undertakings seldom rise above their political genesis. That's a very accurate rule. It can never be avoided.

While today in the Reagan administration, and yesterday in the Carter administration, our political objectives are clear, our strategy is very turgid. The strategy by which you execute these political decisions is, in my opinion, lacking. It doesn't give us a clear sense of direction. I have one view of why this is the case. I have to tell you, before I describe that view to you, that I probably stand alone or am among a very few people who hold the view. Most of my peers, most of my colleagues do not share what I am about to tell you. I told the same thing to the Congress in the course of my testimony on General Jones' proposal for reorganizing the Joint Staff; I want to share those views with you. It is my firm conviction that if you take all the people wearing uniform in the armed forces of the United States, you can separate them into two separate groups of people--one group is responsible for, and on a day-to-day basis does the job of procuring weapons, weapon systems, equipment, and support for the armed forces and of convincing the distributors of public funds that we ought to buy those things. Included in that group are the service chiefs, that is to say the chief of naval operations, chief of staff of the Army, chief of staff of the Air Force. That group has a constituency that is variously described as "iron majors" or "action officers." The relationship between the constituency and the service chiefs is described as the "tyranny of the action officer" or the "tyranny of the iron majors." The constituency is constantly grading the service chiefs, on how skillful they are in acquiring things--battleships, aircraft carriers, airplanes, tanks, MX missiles, Bl bombers, or whatever.

The other group of people, on the other hand, and I include myself in the other group, are the people that have to solve today's problems with today's assets and have to carry out today's political decisions and achieve today's political objectives with the assets that we have at hand. No matter what we might think about the procurement programs that the other group, the service chiefs, are working on we still have to solve today's problems. If we have to fight today, we fight with today's forces, and we had better damn well plan on how best to use today's forces to fight or how to use today's forces to achieve political objectives, because if we don't we are in big trouble.

Constantly we are called upon to tell the political leadership what we would do if such and such a thing happened. Whenever we try to tell the political leadership what we would do, in other words describe our strategy, we are constantly coming head to head with the procurement officials, the service chiefs who say, "No, if you tell them that, we will jeopardize our potential for buying the aircraft carriers, or buying the B1 bomber, or buying the MX missiles. Therefore, you cannot convey that as your strategy to the political leadership." Those of us who are brave enough say, "Well, we are going to do it anyway." But we're constantly battling this procurement strategy. The group that's in the procurement side of the house insist that we follow a procurement strategy, a strategy best designed to enhance the sale of programs that they want to sell to the Congress or they want to sell to the President or they want to sell to the Office of Management and Budget.

The operators, on the other hand, have no constituency. There is nobody grading us except the political leadership at the very top. Normally, success is not noticed, nor should it be, but failure certainly is. And these constant battles between the operators and the procurement people are really deleterious to this nation. It is because of these battles that we do not have a clearly articulated comprehensive strategy of the type that Mahan articulated back in his day. It is a tragedy, but that's the way it is.

I think, in fact I'm firmly convinced, that if General Jones' proposals are accepted and acted upon by Congress it will improve things somewhat. That's not to say that the system doesn't work, it does work, we make it work, but it could be better.

I think most of you are aware that Alfred Thayer Mahan is probably the only synthesist that we have had in recent history. Alfred Thayer Mahan, wrote The Influence of Sea Power Upon History, that was so influential in a certain period in our history. It still is. It influenced the Japanese to do what they did in and prior to World War II, and the Germans to do what they did. He was a synthesist. He could take the pieces of a puzzle and put them all together and make something out of it.

Today there are few if any synthesists in the country, at least in my profession, or in the political world. Most of the people that influence the decisionmakers in this nation, particularly in the political and military fields, are analysts, like myself. They can take a watch apart and lay all the pieces out on the table but they can't put it back together. The ascendency of the analyst, which I hope is behind us, is a fairly well discredited one in the wake of the Falkland Islands. The analyst's power over the political decision making process is far more than it should have been. And, I say this as an analyst; we have done great harm in the process. Normally we start with the answer and work backwards to provide supporting analysis for something we've decided in advance. It's really bad. But Mahan left us with a legacy that we had to live with because no others have come behind him to supply it.

Barbara Tuchman the noted historian whom I admire greatly, wrote an article recently in the Adelphi Papers of the London Institute of International and Strategic Studies in which she took Mahan to task for leading the nation down a very costly trail after the Theodore Roosevelt administration. She took the position that if Mahan had not existed we would not have made all the "mistakes" that occurred during the Theodore Roosevelt regime. I don't agree with her on that. I don't agree with her that Mahan is all bad because he taught the Japanese how to use sea power, because he taught the Germans how to use sea power, and because he taught Theodore Roosevelt how to take advantage of sea power and buy all the expensive battleships and acquire all the territory that led the United States to become a colonial power before World War II. Mahan didn't influence all that. What Mahan was doing was merely describing what was important to the United States as it entered the industrial age, identifying vital interests and showing how sea power could be used to defend those interests.

There are two types of control that the presidency exerts over the military. One is employed in crisis management, the other in war. And they have a different character. The accountable authorities are the same, the President remains accountable, but the type of control that the presidency exercises over the military is different. It's very important for the execution of crisis management or in employing of the military power of the United States to influence events that endanger the United States in a crisis, that the President be tightly in control and know exactly what his military force does so that we are not guilty of making a miscalculation that might result in war. We do not do anything that is not a well conceived step calculated to achieve whatever political objective the President has in mind. Therefore his control has to be very, very tight, and command and control of equipment and capability must be complete.

In war, on the other hand, direction has to be looser and has to be based upon broad political objectives, broad political decisions. And the military must be allowed to do their job the best way they know how, to use their forces the best way they know how to achieve their greatest effect on behalf of the nation.

The British showed us the way in the Falkland Islands—they've continually shown us the way over the years. In the Falkland Islands, the way the British fought that campaign was to give to Admiral Woodward broad political direction and let him fight the battle with his inadequate forces the best way he could.

They won; they won because they achieved their political objectives. You don't decide who wins and loses a war by deciding how many ships, aircraft, or people one side lost as opposed to the other. You ascertain who won the war by deciding who achieved their political objectives. The British clearly achieved their political objectives, right or wrong, in the Falkland Islands. They won the war. They achieved their political objectives because of a great deal of personal heroism, an immense amount of professionalism on the part of their people, using inadequate equipment and deriving a hundred and fifty per cent out of each airplane, ship, and man, and overcoming insurmountable obstacles. There was not a whole lot of confidence over who was going to win that war.

They also did not flinch when they took some very heavy losses. They didn't flinch when they lost the Sheffield, they didn't flinch when they lost the Antelope, they didn't flinch when they lost the other two destroyers, and they didn't flinch when they lost the two landing ships, and they didn't flinch when they lost that large merchant ship the Atlantic Conveyer with all their helicopters on it. They stayed in there and they achieved their political objectives, for which I have the utmost admiration. I'm not sure that we could have pulled it off to that extent. I think we probably would have flinched after we lost the first ship.

Having said that, I would like to point out that the political leadership in the United Kingdom caused the problem. They salvaged it, but they caused the problem by allowing another major nation to so miscalculate the political will and the maritime capability of the United Kingdom that they would challenge them in an area such as the Falkland Islands. President Galtieri and Admiral Anaya clearly miscalculated the British reaction to the Argentine occupation of the Falkland Islands. That miscalculation really started back in the British Ministry of Defense in 1966 when the British decided to move out of the area east of Suez, and subsequently decided to inactivate aircraft carriers and to cut back the size of the Royal Navy. All of these things contributed to the mindset on the part of General Galtieri and Admiral Anaya which led them to believe that, if they went in and took the Falkland Islands, the British lacked the political will to do something about it, and lacked the maritime capability to do something about it. They were wrong.

Now, I want to tell you a little bit about what I do within this umbrella of political authority because it does bear on the problem and it enters closely into the discussion. My role is a maritime role, as I'm sure you are all aware. I've been asked by some relatively hostile questioners if I didn't feel guilty over asking the Congress for so much, when I testified, in order to develop the confidence that I would have a comfortable margin to win a war that will probably never occur. That question lacks sophistication. And the reason it lacks sophistication is that it fails to recognize that the primary purpose of a maritime force to a maritime nation, such as the United States, is to defend its vital interests in peacetime and to deter war. And if you do not maintain a sufficient force to defend your vital interests in peacetime you are then surely going to encounter that which we describe as "war."

The United States is dependent upon the seas for the importation of energy, we are not self-sufficient in energy, yet. We are dependent upon the seas for the importation of the raw materials we we use in our industrial process. And we depend upon the seas to trade with our trading partners. We are not self-sufficient in energy, we are not self-sufficient in raw materials, and we are not a closed loop trading community; we have to trade with our partners overseas, specifically Western Europe, Japan, and Australia. Therefore we need to use the seas and we need to ensure that where our vital interests are threatened--our vital interests mean an access to resources, access to markets, access to energy, access to our friends and allies--we have to use the seas and we must have the maritime power to do so. We must not be challenged either in peacetime or in war. If we're challenged in peacetime it could well lead to war as it did in the case of the British in the Falkland Islands.

Having said that, my specific missions as the Commander in Chief Atlantic, is to deter war, to protect the vital interests of the United States, (that keeps cropping up,) and to employ peacetime maritime presence to influence events in our favor throughout the world. Then, of course, if deterrence fails, I have to do a number of very complex things with the forces that I have available to me today. Those things are to establish a sea bridge between the United States and Western Europe, over which the reinforcement and resupply material will flow. This constitutes the essential strength of the North Atlantic Treaty Organization. Second, to place the cork in the bottle, if you will, in the Greenland/Iceland/United Kingdom gap--that's the water space between Greenland and the U.K.--which will prevent the Soviet Northern fleet from leaving their bases in the north and entering the maritime battleground in the North Atlantic. Third, to establish a sea bridge the entire length of the South Atlantic that will assure we can continue to gain access to our raw materials in Africa and our oil from Nigeria and the Middle East. And finally, to support the adjacent military commanders, specifically General Rogers in Europe and Admiral Long in the Pacific by getting forces to the Indian Ocean and getting forces to the Mediterranean.

I understand these tasks, my people understand the tasks. They prepare for them everyday, in exercises, in making plans, in trying to draft strategy that will fulfill those tasks. But, we hope we'll never have to carry out the plans and the strategy.

Our basic strategy, if it can be said that we have a basic strategy, does recognize U.S. and allied dependence upon the sea, and, because we are dependent upon the sea, recognizes our vulnerability to the sea. In allocating assets to do all these things the Congress has to balance a lot of priorities. They have to balance four basic types of procurement--four basic types of appropriations. They have to worry about force structure, that is the number of ships, aircraft, and people. They have to worry about modernization. Do we have modern ships or do we let our old ships, our old aircraft do the job. Do we provide for sustainability, that is, do we buy those things that let us fight for a long time. Or do we place emphasis on initial war fighting capability? All these things do not fit together very well. You have to decide to give up a little here and buy a little there.

Finally, one comment on things that make life difficult for us: faulty illusions or wishful thinking. I am referring to the short war theory. A short war theory, which Casper Weinburger describes in terms of "the short war fallacy," says that the war will be over in six to eight weeks, therefore we don't need a navy to reinforce and resupply Europe or our allies, and we do not need to buy a lot of ammunition to store in forward positions, we don't need to buy a lot of aircraft to replace those we lose. All we need are the forces to fight the first six weeks of the war. If you embrace that theory, you can reduce a defense budget enormously. The only problem is that it may not be our choice. What we have to continually remind the Congress is when you are looking at a conflict, looking at a war, there are really only four possible outcomes. First, that your adversary will capitulate. In the case of the Soviet Union I find that unlikely. Second, that the U.S. will capitulate. That outcome is unthinkable. Third, that the U.S., when it runs out of conventional means to fight, will escalate to nuclear war ourselves because we have nothing else to do and it is the only choice open to us. That is kind of shocking. And fourth, the fourth possible outcome, and the only one that I find satisfactory, is that we continue to fight by conventional means until we can substitute negotiations for conflict.

79

That's the only satisfactory answer. The short war theorists, however, would deny you that option. I know that there are many people, probably people who are in this room, who are intellectually convinced that the short war theory is viable. But for those who are intellectually persuaded to this viewpoint, I have to ask the question, what if you are wrong? If you're wrong, what am I left with? That is a very unsatisfactory set of options.

NARRATOR: Who would like to ask the first question?

QUESTION: According to our newspapers there was a photograph of an Israeli commander for Beruit who, apparently because of political dissent resigned his command. The article went on to say that he had not been cashiered by the military, he was simply resigning the command that he had had previously. You mentioned that your commanding officers, apparently the Chiefs of Staff, forbid you, at least by implication, to take a stand before Congress that might not be directly in line with their thinking. I'm curious as to what your experience has been as to the limits of the political dissent where you can remain an effective element of the military and still dissent from the political directives of your commanding officers?

ADMIRAL TRAIN: In the case I was referring to where I testified relative to my support of General Jones' proposal, General Jones was still on active duty and was the Chairman of the Joint Chiefs of Staff and would have been very difficult for me to have pressure not to support him even though the Navy as a body disagreed with him violently. But that doesn't really answer your question. I have never, ever been told what I can say or what I cannot say in my dealings with Congress. I have been told what I can't say to the press and that's understandable because the military has to speak with a single voice and we do have to close ranks to the extent that we don't lie to the press, we never do that, but I have been given directions with regard to the press. But never have I been told what to tell the Congress.

The Carter administration was pretty good in spite of the highly publicized case of that Army General in Korea, I can't think of his name now, whom President Carter fired because of his criticism of administrative policies relating to U.S. presence in Korea. That was sort of a rarity. The Carter administration was very careful not to tell us what to say. The case of the Army General was not testimony before Congress, it was a speech given to an army association.

The Reagan administration is very good. I don't know whether it is because they are not paying attention or whether they don't want to tell us, but we are quite free to speak up. Our allies are not, that's an important point. In my dealings with our NATO allies, very few of the military people can say anything in the political force of

NATO. Only the U.S. chairman of the JCS and the Norwegian Chief of Defense, in the four years that I had been with with the military committee, have been able to speak without getting their comments cleared at a higher level. Everybody else does, and the result is that they say nothing. We're in pretty good shape in this regard, and we all know it, all those wearing a uniform know it, and we take great pains not to abuse it. My earlier critical comments dealt with the development of strategy within the organization.

QUESTION: I wonder if you can elaborate on your statement that you think that the U.S. authorities would have flinched in a situation comparable to the British in the Falklands?

ADMIRAL TRAIN: I think that in that type of environment where the British political authorities were telling the military to achieve a broad political objective in the Falkland Islands, that the political leadership of the United Kingdom took great political risks by allowing that operation to continue after they lost the Sheffield. There was such great hue and cry from the people of the United Kingdom about this loss that it took a tremendous amount of bravery to let their forces continue fighting, particularly because they didn't have the things they needed to fight: they didn't have tactical air recon- naissance, they didn't have tactical air support, they were fighting with one arm tied behind their back. I am reasonably convinced that in our own political environment here the pressures would have been such, as we saw demonstrated in Vietnam, the pressures would have been such that had we lost the Sheffield--maybe we could have lost one more ship before we exceeded the threshold of intolerance, but that would have been it. Then we would have had to pull clear.

QUESTION: Do you think that would have also been one of the reasons why the Tehran operation was aborted?

ADMIRAL TRAIN: There is that possibility but I don't really think so. I think that was more mechanical than it was political. There was the fear of failure; that was certainly there, the fear of failure. The command on the scene certainly feared failure. He didn't have that willingness to take a risk for a big gain.

When I went to submarine school many long years ago one of the things my instructors tried to convey to us--and this was not too long after World War II, most of our instructors were World War II submarine skippers--they were trying to convey to us, untrained and unformed students, how you survive and how you can be effective in a combative environment. They all felt to a man that the way you survive in the submarine environment is to attack and attack and attack and bore in. The first exam that we took had a question that clearly addressed this question of survival and tried to convey to us that if you didn't attack, that if you weren't on the offensive, you were going to die. That if you pulled everything down and tried to hide, your life is going to be very short. I've never forgotten that. These same things apply, perhaps, to the Tehran operation. I don't know if I would have made the same decision had I been on the scene or not. But there may have been that element in question. Do they ever know?

QUESTION: On the question of articulating objectives, Admiral Rickover made the point a few weeks ago about the problem of turnover at the policy level of the secretary, the presidency, senior military commanders, and very short periods of time for people in positions compared to the Soviet system. Particularly in the maritime area, the same leaders stay with their naval forces a long, long time.

ADMIRAL TRAIN: Twenty-five years.

QUESTION: Would you comment on that question of the turnover and the ability to carry out a strategy over a long period of time?

ADMIRAL TRAIN: Admiral Rickover has made this point for many years. I've known Admiral Rickover personally since 1950, and he has consistently voiced that opinion. He's more or less right; when I say he's right I don't think he's right to the extent that we should keep command officers aboard submarines for five years. We do that now. Our submarine commanding officers command their ships for about five years--that is too long. I'm unusual in that I have been, in my thirty-three years in the Navy, in two jobs four years. I've been in this job for four years and I was an engineer on a submarine for four years. That is perhaps a little too long but a three year tour length would be extremely useful to all of us and we don't get that. The turnover on a ship--a non-nuclear ship--is such that you lose about half of your crew every year. About fifty percent of your crew will leave every year and be replaced. That's too much. You lose a great deal of expertise and lose continuity and some people never learn their job before they are transferred elsewhere. And that's bad. Now on my own staff there is only one officer that is there today that was there when I arrived four years ago. In many positions on my staff and in key positions, there have been three or four people.

It is a valid criticism and you can do much more towards meeting that criticism than we are today. But we have thousands of excuses for not doing it--mostly invalid. But he's right. He's right on a lot of things--he's wrong on a lot of things, too.

QUESTION: Speaking of subjective information going to the President because a situation might arise when the procurement officers are taking a certain point of view, is the President aware of this?

ADMIRAL TRAIN: No, they don't understand this.   In fact the people that are guilty of it don't understand it.

QUESTION: You have seen this before.   The President sometimes received information that others want him to receive.   That's the simplification of what happens.

ADMIRAL TRAIN: Let me go back to the Iran thing.   I was not involved in it, they didn't even inform me that they were doing it. But, on the Iran hostage raid, on the planning, the case could be made that that was a four-service operation because each service wanted to show that their equipment was important and their role was important, and their mission was important; and they wanted to be involved.   I think that case could be relatively easily made.   Now whether the people that influenced the planning knew they were doing the roles and mission thing, I don't know.   It could well be unconscious.   I'm sure the President didn't know that that was what was happening.   In an ideal world that operation could have been conducted solely by the Marines, or solely with the 82nd Airborne, or any single service.   It probably would have been a more coherent operation had it been done that way.

Let us go back further in time to a safer subject, the Mayaguez crisis back in 1975 where the U.S. merchant ship Mayaguez was taken over by the Cambodians.   They took the ship to an island there off Cambodia and then the crew disappeared.   President Ford decided to do something right away and we once again picked up a force made up of Air Force helicopters, U.S. Marines, and Navy ships, and put them all together real fast and sent them.   They clearly achieved their political objective, they got the crew back, but we lost a lot of people in the process.   We lost a lot of people because we really hadn't exercised very well in making a landing in the face of fire and we made mistakes in using helicopters to get our marines off the ground.   We lost a couple of helicopters; we lost all our radios which were all concentrated on one of those helicopters.   There were a lot of people left on the ground that we couldn't get out of there until we got our tactical air support effort organized.   I worry a little bit about this, but we still achieved our political objective.   But I am not really optimistic that anything will happen because of my own expressed concerns.

QUESTION: What do you think of the possibility of General Jones' suggestions being achieved?

ADMIRAL TRAIN: I think very low.   I did not think so until I testified before the commiittee, but the committee is not really aggregating what they're hearing.   I've had my people present at almost all of the hearings and my people come back and tell me what witnesses said and I can aggregate it quite well.   I can put all this together and figure out about what the sense of the body of witnesses is. The committee apparently can't. I appeared fairly late in the testifying process and the questions they asked me would indicate that either the committee was not listening to the people that went before me or that they didn't have the capability of taking all those inputs and aggregating them into some coherent idea. So I don't think they're up to the task of meeting the challenge that General Jones laid in front of them, which is sad because for the first time we have this opportunity to act from within, from a stimulus that comes from within the organization, from an accountable official who spent four years as a service chief and four years as chairman, who was supported by eight unified commanders, all of us, and two of the service chiefs. And if we don't do it it's a crime. As I say, it's not that the system we have is unsatisfactory; it's not, it works. But it can work better. If we don't do it now, within two or three or four years we'll have another blue ribbon panel come in and tell us how to do it. And it's probably not going to be as good a solution as General Jones's solution.

QUESTION: Would it be more of a political issue if the military, industrial, congressional arm triangles were operating on the side of constituency?

ADMIRAL TRAIN: I haven't seen industry's voice in this expressed, except to the extent that there are retired officers who are now associated with industry, like Tom Moorer, who testified. Now Tom Moorer testified in opposition to my view, which was: "don't do it." But I haven't seen the industrial pressures being brought to bear and I'm not sure they're there, but they could be.

QUESTION: When the Law of the Sea Treaty was being put up for ratification, two articles in the paper said that the rights that guaranteed us free passage offset the disadvantages of it. Now that the United States has chosen not to ratify that treaty, are there dangers that our rights of free passage will be denied.

ADMIRAL TRAIN: Yes, there are. There are three elements in the treaty that were important to nations with maritime interests: they were the right of free passage--the word "free" is important--free passage of international straits, free passage through archipelagoes, and innocent passage of territorial waters. Those three features are what we describe as the security features, the national security features of the treaty. All other regimes were not directly related to our security although they reflected national interests distinctly. In all the other regimes of the Law of the Sea Treaty we could have achieved our objectives by unilateral legislation: the protection of fisheries and the protection of offshore resources, the pollution regime, the oceanographic research--everything else, all the regimes in that treaty, we could protect our interests through unilateral

84

legislation. But, the only ones that we required the entire world to cooperate in were the three I emphasized--free passage of the international straits, free passage of archpelagoes, and the innocent passage of territorial waters. Since part of the treaty extends the territorial seas from three miles to twelve miles the strait passage became even more important. Therefore we thought very strongly that we could take a great deal of pain in the other regimes just to ensure that we achieve those rights of passage. And because of that we tried to persuade the political leadership that the potential losses from the deep sea mining regime, as it was worded in the treaty, could be accommodated. And that if we were not a party to the treaty, the deep sea mining would take place anyway among those countries that were signatories of the treaty. We would gain nothing but we would have lost the strait passage provisions of the treaty. But we were not successful. They tried to balance all these factors, both political and military, and came out on the side that we not sign the treaty. The President made a campaign promise that he would not be a signatory to the treaty.

The other nations that are interested in free passage are the Soviet Union and the United Kingdom. But if the other nations all sign a treaty and they all grant free passage then I presume that we will be the beneficiaries of that, anyway.

QUESTION: I would like to comment on what I thought actually was probably the most important remark you made and that is the United States does have difficulty, in respect of whatever political leaders there are, to translate political objectives into a long term strategy. Why?

ADMIRAL TRAIN: I don't know why, I really don't. It could be part of the continuity problem, the fact we don't really have sufficient continuity in the leadership to translate our objectives to a strategy. That's entirely possible. It's hard to develop a strategy in four years when you shift from Republican to Democrat to Republican. That may be part of it. But, to be honest, I don't know. If I did know I'd try to do something about it, but I don't know, unless it is this problem of a conflict of interest between those people that are trying to put a strategy together on the military side. That surely contributes to it.

QUESTION: But these are subjects, surely, that transcend political argument.

ADMIRAL TRAIN: Yes, indeed, it does. But we have to talk to somebody in order to develop a strategy, and although we may be able to solve our problems within the military we still have to have some continuity in talking to the distributors of public funds and the political leadership, and that continuity is a little bit sporadic to me.

NARRATOR: I would like to thank you for one of the most remarkably clear, vivid and honest, straightforward Conversations we have heard in this historic place. We are very grateful, Admiral.

CONCLUDING OBSERVATIONS

The main themes of the Miller Center in its Forums and Monticello Conversations remain what they have always been: presidential leadership, organizing policymaking, communications with the public, the international setting and the public philosophy.

The particular series of Forums, the texts of which are contained in this volume, have had as their primary focus three urgent problems: national defense, the economy and civil rights. It is sometimes argued that presidential studies should eschew concern with specific policy areas. Instead presidential scholars should devote themselves to the study of the institutional presidency and to the policymaking process.

The assumption which underlies this volume and all other volumes in The Virginia Papers series is that concern with process and problems constitutes a unity and an inseparable part of a coherent whole. The policymaking process is best studied in the light of urgent problems. Otherwise institutional studies suffer from sterile abstractions and general propositions that are not rooted in political realities.

Moreover, in the turmoil of the 1980's when human survival is at stake it is evasive for the social observer to hide behind his lofty abstractions. It will not do when the people are threatened with nuclear destruction for the political scientist to retreat to his ivy tower and spin ever-more refined theories about conflicts threatening to break into flames. If the political observer shuts himself off from a world in flames he is like those Marxian theorists in Nazi Germany who continued to elaborate and refine revisionist and post-Marxian thoughts as Hitler stood at the gates of power.

In any event, the common aim of those who have contributed to this volume is to reunite theory and practice. It is to bring scholarly observers in closer contact with urgent problems and draw policymakers closer to academic thinkers. The fruitful nature of this dialogue has been apparent to some of us at the Miller Center. It should be even more evident in the present set of papers. The mandate of our donor for the Center was to promote understanding while seeking to contribute to social improvement. The Virgina Papers, and this volume in particular as well as those to follow, undertake to fulfill this worthy purpose.